CLASSIC
DESSERTS

CLASSIC DESSERTS

SENSATIONAL SWEET RECIPES FROM AROUND THE WORLD:
140 DELECTABLE DISHES SHOWN IN 250 STUNNING PHOTOGRAPHS

Edited by Kate Eddison

LORENZ BOOKS

This edition is published by Lorenz Books,
an imprint of Anness Publishing Ltd,
Blaby Road, Wigston,
Leicestershire LE18 4SE

Email: info@anness.com

Web: www.lorenzbooks.com; www.annesspublishing.com

If you like the images in this book and would like to
investigate using them for publishing, promotions or
advertising, please visit our website
www.practicalpictures.com for more information.

Publisher: Joanna Lorenz
Editor: Kate Eddison
Designer: Sarah Rock
Indexer: Diana Lecore
Production Controller: Wendy Lawson
Recipes: Pepita Aris, Catherine Atkinson, Mary Banks,
Alex Barker, Ghillie Başan, Georgina Campbell,
Miguel de Castro e Silva, Carole Clements,
Judith H. Dern, Joanna Farrow, Marina Fillippelli,
Jenni Fleetwood, Christine France, Valentina Harris,
Anja Hill, Bridget Jones, Janet Laurence, Vilma Laus,
Sara Lewis, Elena Makhonko, Maggie Mayhew,
Christine McFadden, Ewa Michalik, Anna Mosesson,
Ann Nicol, Marlena Spieler, Mirko Trenkner,
Christopher Trotter, Suzanne Vandyck,
Sunil Vijayakar, Jenny White, Kate Whiteman,
Biddy White-Lennon, Carol Wilson,
Elizabeth Wolf-Cohen and Annette Yates.
Photographers: Martin Brigdale, Nicki Dowey,
Gus Filgate, Amanda Heywood, William Lingwood,
Craig Robertson and Jon Whitaker.

ETHICAL TRADING POLICY
At Anness Publishing we believe that business should
be conducted in an ethical and ecologically sustainable
way, with respect for the environment and a proper
regard to the replacement of the natural resources
we employ.

As a publisher, we use a lot of wood pulp to make
high-quality paper for printing, and that wood
commonly comes from spruce trees. We are therefore
currently growing more than 750,000 trees in three
Scottish forest plantations: Berrymoss (130 hectares/
320 acres), West Touxhill (125 hectares/305 acres) and
Deveron Forest (75 hectares/185 acres). The forests we
manage contain more than 3.5 times the number of
trees employed each year in making paper for the books
we manufacture.

Because of this ongoing ecological investment
programme, you, as our customer, can have the pleasure
and reassurance of knowing that a tree is being
cultivated on your behalf to naturally replace the
materials used to make the book you are holding.

Our forestry programme is run in accordance with the
UK Woodland Assurance Scheme (UKWAS) and will be
certified by the internationally recognized Forest
Stewardship Council (FSC). The FSC is a non-government
organization dedicated to promoting responsible
management of the world's forests. Certification ensures
forests are managed in an environmentally sustainable and
socially responsible way. For further information about this
scheme, go to www.annesspublishing.com/trees

© Anness Publishing Ltd 2011

A CIP catalogue record for this book is available from
the British Library.

PUBLISHER'S NOTE
Although the advice and information in this book are
believed to be accurate and true at the time of going to
press, neither the authors nor the publisher can accept
any legal responsibility or liability for any errors or
omissions that may be made nor for any inaccuracies
nor for any harm or injury that comes about from
following instructions or advice in this book.

Main front cover image shows Miniature Choc-ices,
for recipe see page 17.

NOTES
Bracketed terms are intended for
American readers.

For all recipes, quantities are given in both
metric and imperial measures and, where
appropriate, in standard cups and spoons.
Follow one set of measures, but not a mixture,
because they are not interchangeable.

Standard spoon and cup measures are level.
1 tsp = 5ml, 1 tbsp = 15ml, 1 cup = 250ml/8fl oz.

Australian standard tablespoons are 20ml.
Australian readers should use 3 tsp in place of
1 tbsp for measuring small quantities.

American pints are 16fl oz/2 cups. American
readers should use 20fl oz/2.5 cups in place of
1 pint when measuring liquids.

Electric oven temperatures in this book are for
conventional ovens. When using a fan oven, the
temperature will probably need to be reduced
by about 10–20°C/20–40°F. Since ovens vary,
you should check with your manufacturer's
instruction book for guidance.

The nutritional analysis given for each recipe is
calculated per portion (i.e. serving or item),
unless otherwise stated. If the recipe gives a
range, such as Serves 4–6, then the nutritional
analysis will be for the smaller portion size,
i.e. 6 servings. The analysis does not include
optional ingredients, such as salt added to taste.

Medium (US large) eggs are used unless
otherwise stated.

Contents

Introduction

Desserts are always popular, whether they are a simple sweet treat to finish off a family meal or an elaborate creation that will impress friends as a dinner-party finale. They can range from the lightest fresh fruit sorbet to the most substantial and indulgent steamed chocolate pudding, with a whole world of delicious options in between.

Today we are spoiled for choice when it comes to ready-made desserts, as they are available in abundance in supermarkets and food stores. However, there is still something unequivocally satisfying about preparing something sweet and delicious yourself. It is guaranteed to end a meal on a high note and can even turn a simple supper into a memorable occasion.

CHOOSING A DESSERT

Your choice of what to serve for dessert will be influenced by the occasion and season, as well as the courses that precede. If you are serving a substantial and hearty main course, you may prefer to make a light and fruity dessert to follow it, or if you have your heart set on a rich and luxurious dessert, you could deliberately pick a light main course so that your guests are not too full to enjoy it! In winter, steaming hot puddings will certainly be appreciated, and in summer people may prefer something refreshing and fruity. With the fabulous selection of recipes in this book, you will never be at a loss for ideas to create a perfectly balanced menu, whatever the time of year, occasion or number of guests.

PREPARATION

The time you have to prepare your dessert may also affect your choice of recipe. Many of the recipes in this book can be prepared a day or two in advance, others can be started early in the day and finished off just before you are ready to serve, while frozen desserts can be made weeks in advance, ready to serve whenever you need an emergency sweet dish. In addition, there are many quick-to-prepare recipes that can be rustled up in a matter of minutes. If you are

BELOW: *Serve tarts such as Bakewell Tart warm with plenty of custard.*

ABOVE: *Creamy rice pudding is excellent when topped with a contrasting tart fruit sauce, such as cherry sauce.*

ABOVE: *Some impressive French classics such as Crème Brûlée are actually quite simple to achieve at home.*

ABOVE: *Presentation is key when making desserts for elegant dinner parties, such as with these simple but beautiful shortcakes.*

catering for a large dinner party it is important to leave yourself plenty of time for preparation, or choose a recipe that can be made in advance, to minimize stress on the night. That way, you can have everything under control, relax and enjoy your meal as much as your guests do.

INTERNATIONAL CLASSICS

Today people enjoy food from a wide range of cuisines, and desserts are no exception. This book contains dishes from all around the globe that have become firm favourites worldwide, including British classics such as Eton Mess and Sticky Toffee Pudding, traditional recipes from the US such as Boston Banoffee Pie and Classic American Creamy Cheesecake, French

dishes such as Crème Brûlée and Tarte Tatin, luxurious Italian treats such as Zabaglione and Tiramisù, South-east Asian sweet bites like Chinese-style Toffee Apples and Caramelized Pineapple in Lemon Grass Syrup, as well as a whole host of world-famous dishes from other countries. All the ingredients should be available in large supermarkets, but where a particular ingredient may be hard to buy, a substitute will be suggested.

HOW TO USE THIS BOOK

The recipes in this book are divided into useful chapters to make it easy to find the type of dessert you are looking for. Each recipe has a full-colour photograph of the finished dish to show you the result you are looking

to achieve. All the recipes have clear step-by-step instructions so that even traditional chef's nightmares, such as soufflés and roulades, will be easy to make and taste delicious. It helps to read the whole recipe through before you start, so that you understand the steps involved and can make sure you have all the tools, equipment and ingredients you will need. The book concludes with a fabulous chapter of tips and techniques that you may find useful for making desserts, including step-by-step advice on making all kinds of pastry, lining tart tins and blind baking; making ice cream and water ices; and preparing a whole host of luxurious sauces that will really set your dessert apart from the usual offerings.

Ice creams and iced desserts

Perfect for balmy summer evenings or to follow a rich and warming main course, frozen desserts will never fail to satisfy your guests. Try something light and fruity, such as Summer Berry Frozen Yogurt, for a refreshing dessert that is low in calories. Alternatively, go for something rich and creamy, such as the classic treat that will please children and adults alike: Ice Cream Sundae with Chocolate Sauce.

Lemon sorbet

Sorbets can be made from any citrus fruit but this is probably the all-time classic sorbet. Refreshingly tangy and yet deliciously smooth, it quite literally melts in the mouth.

SERVES 6

200g/7oz/1 cup caster (superfine) sugar
300ml/¹⁄₂ pint/1¹⁄₄ cups water
4 lemons, well scrubbed
1 egg white

VARIATION
Sorbet can be made from any citrus fruit. Use 300ml/¹⁄₂ pint/1¹⁄₄ cups fresh fruit juice and the pared rind of half the squeezed fruits. Use 4 oranges or 2 oranges and 2 lemons, for orange sorbet. For lime sorbet, combine the rind of 3 limes with the juice of 6.

1 Boil the sugar and water in a pan, stirring until the sugar dissolves. Thinly pare the rind of two lemons straight into the pan. Simmer for 2 minutes without stirring. Take the pan off the heat. Cool, then chill.

2 Add the juice from all the lemons and strain into a shallow freezerproof container, reserving the rind.

3 Freeze for 4 hours until mushy.

4 Beat in a food processor until smooth. Lightly whisk the egg white until it is just frothy. Spoon the sorbet back into the tub, beat in the egg white and freeze for 4 hours.

5 Scoop into bowls or glasses and decorate with the reserved rind.

Nutritional information per portion: Energy 134kcal/571kJ; Protein 0.7g; Carbohydrate 35g, of which sugars 35g; Fat 0g, of which saturates 0g; Cholesterol 0mg; Calcium 19mg; Fibre 0g; Sodium 12mg.

Raspberry sherbet

Sherbets are made in the same way as sorbets but with added milk. This low-fat version is made from raspberry purée blended with sugar syrup and fromage frais, flecked with crushed raspberries.

SERVES 6

175g/6oz/³⁄₄ cup caster (superfine) sugar
150ml/¼ pint/²⁄₃ cup water
500g/1¼ lb/3½ cups raspberries,
    plus extra, to serve
500ml/17fl oz/generous 2 cups virtually
    fat-free fromage frais (low-fat
    cream cheese)

COOK'S TIP

If you intend to make this in an ice cream maker, check your handbook before you begin churning: this recipe makes 900ml/1½ pints/3³⁄₄ cups of mixture. If this is too much for your machine, make it in two batches or by hand.

1 Boil the sugar and water in a pan, stirring until the sugar dissolves. Pour into a jug (pitcher) and cool.

2 Process 350g/12oz/2½ cups of the raspberries to a purée in a food processor or blender, then press through a sieve (strainer) over a bowl. Discard the seeds. Stir the sugar syrup into the purée and chill until cold.

3 Add the fromage frais to the purée and whisk until smooth.

4 Pour the mixture into a freezerproof container and freeze for 4 hours, beating once with a fork, electric whisk or in a food processor. After the 4 hours, beat it again. (If using an ice cream maker, churn the mixture until thick but too soft to scoop, then scrape into a freezerproof container.)

5 Crush the remaining raspberries and add them. Mix lightly then freeze for 2–3 hours until firm. Serve with extra raspberries.

Nutritional information per portion: Energy 276kcal/1181kJ; Protein 11.6g; Carbohydrate 60g, of which sugars 60g; Fat 0.6g, of which saturates 0.3g; Cholesterol 1mg; Calcium 163mg; Fibre 3.1g; Sodium 48mg.

Watermelon ice

This recipe is from Sicily, where ice creams and water ices are some of the greatest in the world. Make sure you use a really ripe watermelon for the best flavour.

SERVES 6–8

500g/1¼ lb watermelon, seeded and skinned

275g/10oz/1¼ cups caster (superfine) sugar

30ml/2 tbsp jasmine flower water or 10ml/2 tsp orange blossom water

115g/4oz dark (bittersweet) chocolate, roughly chopped

40g/1½oz/3 tbsp hulled and skinned pistachio nuts, chopped

115g/4oz/⅔ cup candied pumpkin, diced

5ml/1 tsp ground cinnamon

1 Press the watermelon through a sieve (strainer) into a bowl. Add half the sugar and stir until dissolved. Mix in the jasmine flower or orange blossom water.

2 Scrape the mixture into a mould or freezerproof bowl and freeze, stirring every 10 minutes or so to break up the ice crystals.

3 When the mixture is thick and slushy, stir in the remaining sugar, then the chocolate, nuts, pumpkin and cinnamon. Return to the freezer and continue to freeze until the mixture is solid, about 6–8 hours, stirring occasionally.

4 To serve, dip the mould briefly into hot water to loosen the edges. Spoon into serving dishes.

Nutritional information per portion: Energy 294kcal/1243kJ; Protein 2.1g; Carbohydrate 58.6g, of which sugars 57.7g; Fat 7.3g, of which saturates 2.9g; Cholesterol 1mg; Calcium 52mg; Fibre 1.1g; Sodium 72mg.

Summer berry frozen yogurt

Any combination of summer fruits will work for this dish, as long as they are frozen, because this helps to create a chunky texture. Whole fresh or frozen berries make an attractive decoration.

SERVES 6

**350g/12oz/3 cups frozen summer fruits,
    plus extra to serve**
**200g/7oz/scant 1 cup Greek
    (US strained plain) yogurt**
25g/1oz/¼ cup icing (confectioners') sugar

VARIATION
To make a rich and creamy ice cream, use double (heavy) cream in place of the yogurt. It's a lot less healthy but the taste is irresistible.

1 Put all the ingredients into a food processor and process until combined but still quite chunky. Spoon the mixture into six 150ml/¼ pint/²⁄₃ cup ramekin dishes.

2 Cover each dish with clear film (plastic wrap) and place in the freezer for about 2 hours, or until firm.

3 To turn out the frozen yogurts, dip the dishes briefly in hot water and invert them on to small serving plates. Tap the base of the dishes and the yogurts should come out. Serve immediately, with extra frozen summer fruits.

Nutritional information per portion: Energy 71kcal/295kJ; Protein 2.6g; Carbohydrate 8.5g, of which sugars 8.5g; Fat 3.5g, of which saturates 1.7g; Cholesterol 0mg; Calcium 62mg; Fibre 0.7g; Sodium 28mg.

Blueberry ice cream parfait

Blueberries are the perfect fruit to use for this ice cream due to their intense flavour, though this ice cream can also be made with any soft berry, such as raspberries, blackberries or blackcurrants.

SERVES 4

2 large (US extra large) eggs, separated
115g/4oz/1 cup icing (confectioners') sugar
200g/7oz/1¾ cups blueberries
300ml/½ pint/1¼ cups double (heavy) cream
30ml/2 tbsp aquavit (optional)

VARIATION

This basic recipe can be used with any number of different flavourings, such as the grated rind of 1 orange, 30ml/2 tbsp chopped stem ginger or 30ml/2 tbsp raisins and 30ml/2 tbsp rum.

1 Put the egg yolks and half the sugar in a bowl and whisk together until pale and thick. Beat in three-quarters of the blueberries so that they burst and spread their colour.

2 Whisk the egg whites to form soft peaks, then whisk in the remaining sugar. Fold into the blueberry mixture. Whisk the cream with the aquavit, if using, until it just holds its shape. Fold into the blueberry mixture.

3 Transfer to a mould or freezerproof container and freeze for 6–8 hours, until firm.

4 It should be possible to serve the parfait straight from the freezer. If the berries produced a lot of juice, put the parfait in the refrigerator for 20 minutes to soften slightly. Dip the mould briefly in hot water, then turn out the parfait and decorate with the reserved blueberries.

Nutritional information per portion: Energy 536kcal/2228kJ; Protein 4.9g; Carbohydrate 34.6g, of which sugars 34.6g; Fat 43.1g, of which saturates 25.8g; Cholesterol 198mg; Calcium 96mg; Fibre 1.8g; Sodium 55mg.

Iced cranachan

Here is a twist on traditional cranachan: it is made into an ice cream, and the oatmeal has been caramelized to create a luxurious dessert. It is delicious sprinkled with fresh raspberries.

SERVES 4

375g/13oz/generous 1 ¾ cups caster (superfine) sugar
30ml/2 tbsp water
115g/4oz/1 cup pinhead oatmeal
6 egg whites
200ml/7fl oz/scant 1 cup double (heavy) cream
300ml/½ pint/1¼ cups single (light) cream
fresh raspberries, to decorate

1 Place 115g/4oz/generous ¼ cup sugar and the water in a pan and bring to the boil. Boil without stirring until golden, then stir in the oatmeal. Pour on to an oiled tray. Allow to cool.

2 Crush into pieces using a rolling pin or a mortar and pestle. Whisk the egg whites and the remaining sugar in a bowl over a pan of hot water until the sugar dissolves. Remove from the heat and whisk until cold.

3 Mix the creams together then whisk until they thicken slightly. Fold into the egg mixture and add the oatmeal.

4 Pour into a loaf tin (pan) lined with clear film (plastic wrap), and freeze overnight.

5 To serve, turn out of the tin and peel off the clear film. Using a knife dipped in hot water, cut into slices. Decorate with fresh raspberries.

Nutritional information per portion: Energy 855kcal/3588kJ; Protein 11.1g; Carbohydrate 112.2g, of which sugars 94g; Fat 43.4g, of which saturates 25.8g; Cholesterol 110mg; Calcium 154mg; Fibre 1.7g; Sodium 138mg.

Brown bread ice cream

The secret of a good brown bread ice cream is not to have too many breadcrumbs (which makes the ice cream heavy) and, for the best texture and flavour, to toast them until crisp.

SERVES 6 – 8

115g/4oz/2 cups wholemeal
    (whole-wheat) breadcrumbs
115g/4oz/½ cup soft brown sugar
2 large (US extra large) eggs, separated
30–45ml/2–3 tbsp Irish Cream liqueur
450ml/¾ pint/scant 2 cups
    double (heavy) cream

1 Preheat the oven to 190°C/375°F/ Gas 5. Spread the breadcrumbs out on a baking sheet and toast in the oven for about 15 minutes, or until crisp and browned. Leave to cool.

2 Whisk the sugar and egg yolks until creamy. Beat in the Irish Cream. Whisk the cream until soft peaks form.

3 In a separate bowl, whisk the egg whites until stiff.

4 Sprinkle the breadcrumbs over the beaten egg mixture, add the cream and fold into the mixture with a spoon. Fold in the beaten egg whites. Turn the mixture into a freezerproof container, cover and freeze.

Nutritional information per portion: Energy 561kcal/2332kJ; Protein 6g; Carbohydrate 37.3g, of which sugars 23g; Fat 43.6g, of which saturates 25.7g; Cholesterol 179mg; Calcium 84mg; Fibre 0.4g; Sodium 196mg

Miniature choc-ices

For summer entertaining, these little chocolate-coated ice creams make a fun and impressive alternative to the more familiar store-bought after-dinner chocolates.

MAKES ABOUT 25

750ml/1¼ pints/3 cups vanilla, chocolate or coffee ice cream

200g/7oz plain (semisweet) chocolate, broken into pieces

25g/1oz milk chocolate, broken into pieces

25g/1oz/¼ cup chopped hazelnuts, lightly toasted

COOK'S TIP

If the melted plain chocolate is very runny, leave it for a few minutes to thicken up slightly before spooning it over the ice cream scoops. The milk chocolate can be piped on the choc-ices, using a piping bag fitted with a writing nozzle.

1 Put a large baking sheet in the freezer for 10 minutes. Using a melon baller, scoop balls of the ice cream and place these on the baking sheet. Freeze for at least 1 hour until firm.

2 Line a second baking sheet with non-stick baking parchment and place in the freezer for 15 minutes. Melt the plain chocolate in a heatproof bowl set over a pan of gently simmering water. Melt the milk chocolate in a separate bowl.

3 Transfer the ice cream scoops to the paper-lined sheet.

4 Spoon a little plain chocolate over one scoop of ice cream so that most of it is coated.

5 Immediately sprinkle with chopped nuts, before the chocolate sets. Coat half the remaining scoops in the same way, sprinkling each one with nuts before the chocolate sets. Spoon the remaining plain chocolate over all the remaining scoops.

6 Using a teaspoon, drizzle the milk chocolate over the choc-ices which are not topped with nuts. Freeze again until ready to serve.

Nutritional information per portion: Energy 117kcal/488kJ; Protein 1.8g; Carbohydrate 10.7g, of which sugars 10.6g; Fat 7.7g, of which saturates 4.3g; Cholesterol 1mg; Calcium 36mg; Fibre 0.3g; Sodium 19mg.

Lemon sorbet cups with summer fruits

In this stunning dessert, lemon sorbet is moulded into pretty containers for a selection of summer fruits. Dried tropical fruits such as mango and papaya work just as well.

SERVES 6

500ml/17fl oz/2¼ cups Lemon Sorbet
   (see page 10)
225g/8oz/2 cups strawberries, halved
150g/5oz/scant 1 cup raspberries
75g/3oz/¾ cup redcurrants,
   blackcurrants or whitecurrants
15ml/1 tbsp caster (superfine) sugar
45ml/3 tbsp Cointreau or other
   orange-flavoured liqueur

1 Put six 150ml/¼ pint/⅔ cup metal moulds in the freezer for 15 minutes to chill. At the same time, remove the sorbet from the freezer to soften slightly.

2 Using a teaspoon, pack the sorbet into the moulds, building up a layer about 1cm/½in thick around the base and sides, and leaving a deep cavity in the centre. Hold the moulds in a dish towel as you work. Return each mould to the freezer once lined.

3 Place the fruit in a bowl. Add the sugar and liqueur and toss together lightly. Cover and chill for 2 hours.

4 Once the sorbet has frozen, loosen the edges with a knife, then dip in hot water for 2 seconds. Invert the cups on a tray. Turn them over so they are ready to fill and freeze until required.

5 To serve, place the cups on serving plates and fill with the fruits, spooning over any juices.

Nutritional information per portion: Energy 159kcal/678kJ; Protein 1.4g; Carbohydrate 38.1g, of which sugars 38.1g; Fat 0.1g, of which saturates 0g; Cholesterol 0mg; Calcium 15mg; Fibre 0.8g; Sodium 21mg.

Spiced sorbet pears

Pears poached in wine make an elegant dessert at any time of the year. In this recipe, the pears are hollowed out and filled with a wine-and-pear-flavoured sorbet. Start the day before.

SERVES 6

600ml/1 pint/2½ cups red wine

2 cinnamon sticks, halved

115g/4oz/generous ½ cup caster (superfine) sugar

6 plump pears, peeled, with stalks still attached

1 Heat the wine, cinnamon and sugar in a pan, until the sugar dissolves. Stand the pears in the pan, cover and simmer gently for 10–20 minutes until tender, turning occasionally.

2 Remove the pears and set aside to cool. Boil the juices to reduce to 350ml/12fl oz/1½ cups. Cool. Cut a 2.5cm/1in slice off the top of each pear as a lid and reserve. Use an apple corer to remove the cores.

3 Scoop out the centre of each pear and reserve. Put the pears and lids in the freezer. Strain the juices, set 75ml/ 5 tbsp aside and put the rest in a food processor with the flesh. Blend well.

4 Pour into a freezerproof container and freeze for 4 hours, beating twice. Spoon the sorbet into the pears, add the lids and freeze overnight. Stand at room temperature for 30 minutes before serving with the reserved syrup.

Nutritional information per portion: Energy 198kcal/835kJ; Protein 0.6g; Carbohydrate 35.2g, of which sugars 35.2g; Fat 0.2g, of which saturates 0g; Cholesterol 0mg; Calcium 33mg; Fibre 3.3g; Sodium 12mg.

Coconut and passion fruit Alaska

Baked Alaska lends itself to many variations on a basic theme. This version comprises passion fruit, coconut sponge, passion fruit ice cream and delicious coconut-flavoured meringue.

SERVES 8

1 litre/1¾ pints/4 cups passion fruit
   ice cream
60ml/4 tbsp Kirsch
3 passion fruit
3 egg whites
115g/4oz/generous ½ cup caster
   (superfine) sugar
50g/2oz/½ cup creamed coconut, grated

FOR THE SPONGE

115g/4oz/½ cup unsalted butter, softened
115g/4oz/generous ½ cup caster (superfine) sugar
2 eggs
115g/4oz/1 cup self-raising (self-rising) flour
2.5ml/½ tsp baking powder
5ml/1 tsp almond extract
40g/1½ oz/½ cup desiccated
   (dry unsweetened shredded) coconut
15ml/1 tbsp milk

1 Preheat the oven to 180°C/350°F/Gas 4. Grease and line an 18cm/7in round cake tin (pan). Put all the sponge ingredients in a bowl and whisk until smooth. Spoon into the prepared tin, level the surface and bake for 35 minutes until the sponge is just firm. Leave to cool on a wire rack.

2 Dampen a 1.2 litre/2 pint/5 cup bowl and line it with clear film (plastic wrap). Remove the ice cream from the freezer for 15 minutes to soften slightly. Pack it into the lined bowl and return it to the freezer for 1 hour. Place the sponge on a small baking sheet or ovenproof plate and drizzle the surface with Kirsch. Remove the pulp from the fruit and scoop over the sponge.

3 Dip the bowl with the ice cream into hot water for about 2 seconds to loosen the shaped ice cream. Invert it on to the sponge. Peel away the clear film and put the cake and ice cream in the freezer.

4 Whisk the egg whites in a clean bowl until stiff. Add the sugar a tablespoon at a time, whisking well each time, until the meringue is thick and glossy. Fold in the grated creamed coconut. With a metal spatula, spread the meringue all over the ice cream and sponge. Return to the freezer.

5 About 15 minutes before serving, preheat the oven to 220°C/425°F/Gas 7. Bake for 4–5 minutes, watching closely, until the peaks are golden. Serve immediately.

Nutritional information per portion: Energy 615kcal/2576kJ; Protein 9.5g; Carbohydrate 75.3g, of which sugars 63.1g; Fat 30.9g, of which saturates 20.8g; Cholesterol 111mg; Calcium 189mg; Fibre 1.4g; Sodium 212mg.

Frosted raspberry and coffee terrine

A white chocolate and raspberry layer and a contrasting smooth coffee layer make this attractive looking dessert a doubly delicious treat for grown-up palates.

SERVES 6–8

30ml/2 tbsp ground coffee,
  e.g. mocha orange-flavoured
250ml/8fl oz/1 cup milk
4 eggs, separated
50g/2oz/1/4 cup caster (superfine) sugar
30ml/2 tbsp cornflour (cornstarch)
150ml/1/4 pint/2/3 cup double
  (heavy) cream
150g/5oz white chocolate,
  roughly chopped
115g/4oz/2/3 cup raspberries
shavings of white chocolate and
  unsweetened cocoa powder, to decorate

COOK'S TIP

After decorating, allow the terrine to soften in the fridge for 20 minutes before slicing and serving.

1 Line a 1.5 litre/2$\frac{1}{2}$ pint/6$\frac{1}{4}$ cup loaf tin (pan) with clear film (plastic wrap) and put in the freezer. Put the coffee in a jug (pitcher). Heat 100ml/3$\frac{1}{2}$ fl oz/ scant $\frac{1}{2}$ cup of the milk to near-boiling point, add to the coffee and set aside.

2 Blend the egg yolks, sugar and cornflour together in a pan and whisk in the remaining milk and the cream. Bring to the boil, stirring, until thickened. Divide the hot mixture between two bowls and add the white chocolate to one, stirring until melted. Strain the coffee through a fine sieve (strainer) into the other bowl and mix well. Leave until cool, stirring occasionally.

3 Whisk two of the egg whites until stiff, then fold into the coffee custard. Spoon into the tin and freeze for 30 minutes. Whisk the remaining whites and fold into the chocolate mixture with the raspberries.

4 Spoon into the tin, level and freeze for 4 hours. Turn it out and peel off the clear film. Decorate with chocolate shavings and cocoa powder.

Nutritional information per portion: Energy 299kcal/1249kJ; Protein 7g; Carbohydrate 25g, of which sugars 20g; Fat 20g, of which saturates 11g; Cholesterol 143mg; Calcium 121mg; Fibre 0.4g; Sodium 85mg.

Maple coffee and pistachio bombes

Real maple syrup tastes infinitely better than the synthetic varieties and is well worth searching for. Here it sweetens the dark coffee centre of these pretty pistachio bombes.

SERVES 6

FOR THE PISTACHIO ICE CREAM
50g/2oz/$\frac{1}{4}$ cup caster
   (superfine) sugar
50ml/2fl oz/$\frac{1}{4}$ cup water
175g/6oz can evaporated milk, chilled
50g/2oz/$\frac{1}{2}$ cup shelled and skinned
   pistachio nuts, finely chopped
drop of green food colouring (optional)
200ml/7fl oz/scant 1 cup whipping cream

FOR THE MAPLE COFFEE CENTRES
30ml/2 tbsp ground coffee
150ml/$\frac{1}{4}$ pint/$\frac{2}{3}$ cup single
   (light) cream
50ml/2fl oz/$\frac{1}{4}$ cup maple syrup
2 egg yolks
5ml/1 tsp cornflour (cornstarch)
150ml/$\frac{1}{4}$ pint/$\frac{2}{3}$ cup whipping cream

1 Put six 175ml/6fl oz/$\frac{3}{4}$ cup mini pudding basins or dariole moulds into the freezer to chill. Put the sugar and water in a pan and heat gently until dissolved. Bring to the boil and simmer for 3 minutes. Allow to cool.

2 Stir in the chilled evaporated milk, pistachio nuts and colouring, if using. Lightly whip the cream until it forms soft peaks and blend into the mixture. Pour the mixture into a freezerproof container and freeze for at least 2 hours. Whisk it until smooth, then freeze for 2 hours until frozen, but not solid.

3 Put the coffee in a jug (pitcher). Heat the cream to near-boiling point and pour over the coffee. Leave for 4 minutes. Whisk the maple syrup, egg yolks and cornflour together. Strain over the coffee cream, whisking. Return to the pan and cook gently, stirring, for 1–2 minutes, until thick. Leave to cool, stirring often.

4 Meanwhile, line the moulds with the ice cream, keeping the thickness even. Freeze until firm again. Beat the cream until peaks form, then fold into the custard. Spoon into the moulds. Cover and freeze for 2 hours. Serve immediately.

Nutritional information per portion: Energy 436kcal/1807kJ; Protein 7g; Carbohydrate 21g, of which sugars 19g; Fat 37g, of which saturates 21g; Cholesterol 152mg; Calcium 164mg; Fibre 0.4g; Sodium 116mg.

Layered chocolate and chestnut bombes

*These delicious bombes look very effective served on plates drizzled with melted plain chocolate.
Or simply dust the plates with cocoa powder or sprinkle the bombes with grated chocolate.*

SERVES 6

3 egg yolks
75g/3oz/6 tbsp caster (superfine) sugar
10ml/2 tsp cornflour (cornstarch)
300ml/½ pint/1¼ cups milk
115g/4oz plain (semisweet) chocolate, broken
 into pieces, plus 50g/2oz, to decorate

150g/5oz/½ cup sweetened chestnut purée
30ml/2 tbsp brandy or Cointreau
130g/4½ oz/generous ½ cup mascarpone
5ml/1 tsp vanilla extract
450ml/¾ pint/scant 2 cups double
 (heavy) cream

1 In a bowl, whisk the egg yolks, sugar, cornflour and a little milk. Bring the remaining milk to the boil in a heavy pan. Pour the milk over the egg mixture, whisking well. Return to the pan and cook gently, stirring, until thickened, but do not boil. Divide the custard equally among three bowls.

2 Add 115g/4oz of the chocolate to one bowl and stir until melted and smooth. If it fails to melt completely, microwave very briefly.

3 If the chestnut purée is firm, beat until soft and stir into the second bowl, with the brandy or Cointreau. Add the mascarpone and vanilla extract to the third bowl. Cover each closely with a circle of baking parchment and leave to cool.

4 Whip the cream into soft peaks and fold one-third into each of the custard mixtures. Share the chestnut mixture between six 150ml/¼ pint/⅔ cup plain or fluted moulds and level the surface.

5 Spoon the chocolate mixture over the chestnut mixture in the moulds and level the surface. Spoon the vanilla mixture over the chocolate. Cover and freeze for 6 hours or overnight.

6 To serve, melt the chocolate for decoration in a heatproof bowl over a pan of gently simmering water. Transfer to a paper piping bag and snip off the tip; alternatively use a piping bag fitted with a writing nozzle. Scribble lines of melted chocolate over the serving plates to decorate. Loosen the edge of each mould with a knife, dip very briefly in hot water, then invert on to a flat surface. Using a metal spatula, transfer the bombes to the serving plates. Leave for 10 minutes at room temperature before serving.

Nutritional information per portion: Energy 671kcal/2786kJ; Protein 7.9g; Carbohydrate 40.2g, of which sugars 31.1g; Fat 53.1g, of which saturates 31.7g; Cholesterol 217mg; Calcium 133mg; Fibre 1.5g; Sodium 48mg.

Chocolate teardrops with cherry sauce

These sensational chocolate cases are surprisingly easy to make. Once filled, they freeze well, making them the perfect choice for a special occasion dessert.

SERVES 6

90g/3½ oz plain (semisweet) chocolate, broken into pieces
115g/4oz amaretti
300ml/½ pint/1¼ cups whipping cream
2.5ml/½ tsp almond extract
30ml/2 tbsp icing (confectioners') sugar
6 pairs of fresh cherries, to decorate

FOR THE SAUCE

2.5ml/½ tsp cornflour (cornstarch)
75ml/5 tbsp water
225g/8oz/2 cups fresh cherries, pitted and halved
45ml/3 tbsp caster (superfine) sugar
10ml/2 tsp lemon juice
45ml/3 tbsp gin

1 Cut out six Perspex (Plexiglass) strips, each measuring 27 x 3cm/ 10½ x 1¼in. Melt the chocolate in a heatproof bowl over a pan of simmering water. Remove from the heat and leave for 5 minutes. Line a baking sheet with baking parchment.

2 Coat one side of a Perspex strip by dipping it in the chocolate, apart from 1cm/½in at each end. Bring the ends together, with the coated side on the inside. Secure the ends with a paper clip. Put on the baking sheet. Repeat with the other five. Chill until set. Crush the amaretti with a rolling pin.

3 Whip the cream, almond extract and icing sugar until thick but soft. Fold in the biscuits. Use to fill the chocolate cases. Tap the baking sheet gently on the work surface to level the filling. Freeze for 3 hours or overnight.

4 In a pan, stir the cornflour and a little water to a paste. Stir in the remaining water, cherries, sugar and lemon juice. Bring to the boil, stirring until thickened. Remove from the heat and leave to cool. Stir in the gin.

5 Remove the paper clips and peel off the Perspex. Serve with a little sauce, decorated with pairs of cherries.

Nutritional information per portion: Energy 441kcal/1839kJ; Protein 3.3g; Carbohydrate 45g, of which sugars 36.1g; Fat 26.9g, of which saturates 16.3g; Cholesterol 53mg; Calcium 72mg; Fibre 1.1g; Sodium 78mg.

Chocolate millefeuille slice

This stunning dessert can be prepared days in advance, ready to impress dinner guests. Simply transfer it to the refrigerator about 30 minutes before serving so that it's easier to slice.

SERVES 8

4 egg yolks
10ml/2 tsp cornflour (cornstarch)
300ml/1/2 pint/11/4 cups milk
175ml/6fl oz/3/4 cup maple syrup
250ml/8fl oz/1 cup crème fraîche
115g/4oz/1 cup pecan nuts, chopped

TO FINISH

150g/5oz plain (semisweet) chocolate, melted, plus 50g/2oz pared into thin curls
300ml/1/2 pint/11/4 cups double (heavy) cream
45ml/3 tbsp icing (confectioners') sugar
30ml/2 tbsp brandy (optional)
lightly toasted pecan nuts

1 In a bowl, whisk the egg yolks, cornflour and a little milk until smooth. Pour the remaining milk into a pan, bring to the boil, then add to the yolk mixture, stirring.

2 Return to the pan and stir in the maple syrup. Cook gently, stirring until thick and smooth. Do not boil. Pour into a bowl and cover closely with baking parchment. Cool.

3 Stir in the crème fraîche and pour into a shallow freezerproof container. Freeze for 3–4 hours, beating twice. Add the pecan nuts. Freeze overnight.

4 On baking parchment, draw four 19 x 12cm/71/2 x 41/2in rectangles. Spoon melted chocolate on to each rectangle and leave to set.

5 Whip the cream, icing sugar and brandy into soft peaks. Peel the paper from a chocolate rectangle and place on a freezerproof plate.

6 Spread one-third of the cream on the chocolate. Top with scoops of ice cream. Cover with a chocolate rectangle. Repeat the layers, finishing with chocolate. Top with pecan nuts and chocolate curls. Freeze until firm.

Nutritional information per portion: Energy 667kcal/2772kJ; Protein 6.7g; Carbohydrate 43.3g, of which sugars 42.6g; Fat 53.1g, of which saturates 27.2g; Cholesterol 191mg; Calcium 117mg; Fibre 1.3g; Sodium 99mg.

Ice cream sundae with chocolate sauce

This immensely popular dessert consists of good quality vanilla ice cream lavishly drizzled with a decadent warm Belgian chocolate sauce. The topping is up to the individual, but whipped cream, chopped nuts, chocolate chips, and a wafer can all be added. Make it at least a day ahead.

MAKES 10

350ml/12fl oz/1¹/₂ cups full cream (whole) milk
250ml/8fl oz/1 cup double (heavy) cream
1 vanilla pod (bean)
4 egg yolks
100g/3³/₄oz/¹/₂ cup caster (superfine) sugar
sweetened whipped cream, chopped nuts,
    chocolate chips and ice cream wafers,
    to serve (optional)

FOR THE CHOCOLATE SAUCE

60ml/4 tbsp double (heavy) cream
150ml/¹/₄ pint/²/₃ cup milk
250g/9oz Callebaut callets (semisweet bits) or
    other good-quality Belgian chocolate, cut into
    small pieces
15ml/1 tbsp brandy, rum or liqueur,
    such as Grand Marnier (optional)

1 First make the ice cream. Pour 250ml/8fl oz/1 cup of the milk into a heavy pan. Add the cream. Slit the vanilla pod down its length, scrape the seeds into the pan with the tip of the knife, then heat the mixture. When it is hot, but not boiling, remove it from the heat and leave to stand for 10 minutes.

2 Meanwhile, mix the egg yolks and sugar in a bowl and beat for 5 minutes, until thick and creamy. Still beating, add one-third of the warm milk mixture in a steady stream. Pour in the remaining milk mixture and whisk for 2 minutes.

3 Return the mixture to the pan and cook over medium-high heat, stirring constantly, for 5–7 minutes, until the custard is thick enough to coat the back of a spoon. Immediately remove the pan from the heat and stir in the remaining milk. Strain the custard into a stainless steel or glass bowl set over a bowl of iced water. When it has cooled to room temperature, cover and chill in the refrigerator.

4 Scrape the chilled mixture into a freezer container, cover and freeze until firm, whisking 2 or 3 times. Alternatively, use an ice cream maker, transferring the soft-serve ice cream to a tub and freezing it.

5 Make the chocolate sauce. Mix the cream and milk in a pan and heat to simmering point. Remove from the heat and stir in the chocolate pieces until they melt. Stir in the brandy or liqueur, if using. Pour 20ml/4 tsp of the warm chocolate sauce into each glass. Top with two scoops of ice cream and more of the sauce. Sprinkle with chopped nuts and chocolate chips, or top with a wafer, if you like.

Per portion Energy 930kcal/3869kJ; Protein 11.2g; Carbohydrate 72.3g, of which sugars 71.7g; Fat 68.2g, of which saturates 40.2g; Cholesterol 324mg; Calcium 229mg; Fibre 1.6g; Sodium 80mg.

Rich chocolate mousse gateau

Because this gateau is heavily laced with liqueur, you can easily get away with using a store-bought sponge cake. The mousse is rich, so serve small portions only.

SERVES 12

400g/14oz moist chocolate sponge cake
75ml/5 tbsp Cointreau or other
   orange-flavoured liqueur
finely grated rind and juice of 1 orange
300g/11oz plain (semisweet) chocolate,
   broken into pieces
25g/1oz/¼ cup unsweetened cocoa powder

45ml/3 tbsp golden (light corn) syrup
3 eggs
300ml/½ pint/1¼ cups whipping cream
150ml/¼ pint/⅔ cup double (heavy) cream,
   lightly whipped
unsweetened cocoa powder,
   for dusting

1 Cut the cake into 5mm/¼in thick slices. Set one third aside, and use the remainder to make a case for the mousse. Line the bottom of a 23cm/9in springform or loose-based cake tin (pan) with cake, trimming to fit neatly, then use more for the sides, making a case about 4cm/1½in deep.

2 Mix 30ml/2 tbsp of the liqueur with the orange juice and drizzle over the sponge case.

3 Place the chocolate, cocoa powder, syrup and remaining liqueur in a heatproof bowl over a pan of gently simmering water. Remove when the chocolate melts. Stir until smooth.

4 Whisk the eggs with the orange rind in a mixing bowl until they are thick and pale. Whip the whipping cream until it forms soft peaks.

5 Fold the chocolate mixture into the whisked eggs, using a large metal spoon, then fold in the cream. Scrape the mixture into the sponge case and level the surface.

6 Cover with the reserved chocolate cake, trimming the pieces to fit. Cover and freeze overnight.

7 Transfer the gateau to the refrigerator 30 minutes before serving. Invert on to a plate, spread with the double cream and dust with the unsweetened cocoa powder.

Nutritional information per portion: Energy 488kcal/2032kJ; Protein 6g; Carbohydrate 37.4g, of which sugars 29.6g; Fat 34.4g, of which saturates 15.3g; Cholesterol 92mg; Calcium 61mg; Fibre 1.2g; Sodium 175mg.

Frozen Grand Marnier soufflés

Light and fluffy yet almost ice cream, these delicious soufflés are perfect for a special dinner. Redcurrants or other small, soft fruits make a delicate decoration.

SERVES 8

200g/7oz/1 cup caster (superfine) sugar
6 large (US extra large) eggs, separated
250ml/8fl oz/1 cup milk
15g/½ oz/1 tbsp powdered gelatine,
  soaked in 45ml/3 tbsp cold water
450ml/¾ pint/1⅞ cups double
  (heavy) cream
60ml/4 tbsp Grand Marnier
redcurrants, to decorate

COOK'S TIP
The soft ball stage of a syrup is when a teaspoon of the mixture dropped into a glass of cold water sets into a soft ball.

VARIATION
If you prefer, you can make just one pudding in a large soufflé dish.

1 Wrap a double collar of baking parchment around eight dessert glasses or ramekin dishes and tie with string. Whisk together 75g/3oz/generous ⅓ cup of the caster sugar with the egg yolks, until the yolks are pale. This will take about 5 minutes by hand or about 3 minutes with an electric hand mixer.

2 Heat the milk until almost boiling, then add it to the yolks, whisking constantly. Return to the pan and stir over a gentle heat until the custard is thick enough to coat the back of the spoon. Remove from the heat. Stir in the gelatine. Pour into a bowl and leave to cool. Whisk occasionally, until on the point of setting.

3 Put the remaining sugar in a pan with 45ml/3 tbsp water and dissolve it over a low heat. Bring to the boil and boil rapidly until it reaches the soft ball stage or 119°C/238°F on a sugar thermometer. Remove from the heat. In a clean bowl, whisk the egg whites until stiff. Add the syrup, whisking constantly. Cool.

4 Add the Grand Marnier to the custard. Whisk the cream to form soft peaks and fold into the egg whites, with the custard. Pour into the glasses. Freeze overnight. Remove the parchment, leave at room temperature for 15 minutes and serve.

Nutritional information per portion: Energy 478kcal/1991kJ; Protein 6.7g; Carbohydrate 33.7g, of which sugars 33.7g; Fat 34.9g, of which saturates 20.3g; Cholesterol 222mg; Calcium 99mg; Fibre 0g; Sodium 79mg.

Iced mousse with hot pineapple

This heavenly combination of coconut and pineapple will conjure up thoughts of sun, sea, sand and tropical islands. If you prefer, replace the liqueur with fresh orange juice.

SERVES 6–8

4 large (US extra large) eggs, separated

2.5ml/½ tsp vanilla extract

75g/3oz/generous ⅓ cup caster (superfine) sugar

175ml/6fl oz/¾ cup milk

90ml/6 tbsp coconut milk

1½ sachets powdered gelatine

90ml/6 tbsp coconut liqueur

275ml/9fl oz/generous 1 cup double (heavy) cream

115g/4oz fresh pineapple, grated, juice retained

90–105ml/6–7 tbsp pineapple jam

50g/2oz shredded coconut, toasted

a few pieces of fresh or crystallized pineapple, to decorate

1 Wrap a baking-parchment collar around a 1.2 litre/2 pint/5 cup soufflé dish. Beat together the egg yolks, vanilla and sugar. Bring the milk and coconut milk just to the boil, pour over the yolk mixture, whisking constantly, and return to the pan. Continue whisking over a medium heat until it coats the back of a spoon. Sprinkle on the gelatine, leave for 20 seconds then stir until dissolved.

2 Stir the liqueur into the custard, then place the pan in a bowl of ice to chill. Whip the cream until it stands in peaks and, in another bowl, whisk the egg whites to soft peaks. Fold them both into the custard. Spoon into the prepared dish and leave to set for 2 hours. Freeze the mousse for 2–3 hours.

3 Heat the pineapple and jam in a small pan with 30–45ml/2–3 tbsp water and simmer for 2–3 minutes, stirring. To serve, remove the paper collar from the soufflé and carefully press the toasted coconut against the sides. Decorate the top with pieces of fresh or crystallized pineapple and serve with the hot sauce.

Nutritional information per portion: Energy 373kcal/1556kJ; Protein 6g; Carbohydrate 27g, of which sugars 27g; Fat 25g, of which saturates 15g; Cholesterol 176mg; Calcium 73mg; Fibre 0.6g; Sodium 87mg.

Italian cream and chocolate pudding

This delicious iced pudding, zuccotto, is intended to look like the traditional helmet of a Tuscan mercenary going into battle, which in turn was named after a small, rounded pumpkin.

SERVES 6–8

75g/3oz/¹⁄₂ cup hazelnuts
115g/4oz unsweetened cooking chocolate
ready-made basic sponge cake, about 25cm/10in
90ml/6 tbsp brandy
60ml/4 tbsp amaretto liqueur
1 litre/1³⁄₄ pints/4 cups double (heavy) cream
75g/3oz/¹⁄₂ cup blanched almonds,
    coarsely chopped

30ml/2 tbsp plain (semisweet) chocolate drops
30ml/2 tbsp chopped mixed crystallized
    (candied) peel or glacé (candied) fruits
150g/5oz/1¹⁄₄ cups icing (confectioners') sugar,
    sifted, plus extra for dusting
30ml/2 tbsp unsweetened cocoa powder

1 Lay the hazelnuts out on a baking sheet and toast them under a hot grill (broiler), turning occasionally, for about 5 minutes, or until golden.

2 Hold a few hazelnuts at a time in a dish towel and rub off their skins. Cool and chop, then set aside.

3 Melt the cooking chocolate in a heatproof bowl over a pan of gently simmering water. Remove the bowl from the pan.

4 Take a large bowl (large enough to take all the cake and the cream) and draw a circle slightly larger than the bowl's circumference on a sheet of stiff paper. Cut out the circle and set it aside. Line the bowl with foil.

5 Slice the cake into strips about 4cm/1¹⁄₂in wide, dip each strip in brandy, then in amaretto, and press the strips against the sides of the bowl to line it. Set aside.

6 In a large bowl, whip the cream until stiff peaks form. Fold the hazelnuts, almonds, chocolate drops, crystallized peel or glacé fruits, and sugar into the cream.

7 Transfer half the cream mixture to another bowl. Stir the melted chocolate into one half of the cream.

8 Spoon the white cream over the base and sides of the cake-lined bowl, then use the chocolate cream to fill the hollow in the centre. Level the top with a spatula. Place the bowl in the freezer for at least 3 hours.

9 Meanwhile, fold the circle of paper into eight and cut out four alternate sections.

10 Shortly before serving, turn the zuccotto out on to a platter. Remove the foil carefully and sift over the remaining icing sugar.

11 Lay the cut-out circle of paper on top of the zuccotto. Carefully hold it in place and dust it with the cocoa powder. Remove the paper carefully. You should now have alternate segments of brown and white, which is the traditional design. Serve the zuccotto immediately.

Nutritional information per portion: Energy 1087kcal/4507kJ; Protein 9.9g; Carbohydrate 56.5g, of which sugars 44.8g; Fat 96.3g, of which saturates 45.5g; Cholesterol 233mg; Calcium 147mg; Fibre 2.2g; Sodium 245mg.

Cold puddings

Desserts that can be made in advance and chilled in the refrigerator before serving are great for dinner parties; many of the recipes in this chapter can be prepared quite a few hours ahead. The classic pudding Fruit Trifle is quintessentially British, and lovely served for a summer dessert. French and Italian dishes really come into their own here, with wonderful creamy recipes such as Crème Brûlée, Zabaglione and Tiramisù.

Eton mess

This 'mess' of whipped cream, crushed meringue and strawberries is a real summer classic.
It is quick and easy to prepare, and can be made with any other soft fruit or berries you like.

SERVES 4

450g/1lb ripe strawberries
45ml/3 tbsp elderflower cordial
   or orange liqueur
300ml/½ pint/1¼ cups double
   (heavy) cream
4 meringues or meringue baskets

COOK'S TIPS
You can serve Eton Mess just as it is or
accompanied by crisp sweet biscuits
(cookies), if you like.

1 Remove the green hulls from the strawberries and slice the fruit into a bowl, reserving a few for decoration.

2 Sprinkle with the elderflower cordial or orange liqueur. Cover the bowl and chill for about 2 hours.

3 Whip the cream until soft peaks form. Crush the meringue into small pieces. Add the fruit and most of the meringue to the cream and fold in lightly. Spoon into serving dishes and chill until required. Before serving, decorate with the reserved strawberries and meringue.

Nutritional information per portion: Energy 526kcal/2182kJ; Protein 3.5g; Carbohydrate 32.8g, of which sugars 32.8g; Fat 40.4g, of which saturates 25.1g; Cholesterol 103mg; Calcium 60mg; Fibre 1.4g; Sodium 53mg.

Cranachan

This lovely, nutritious dish is based on a traditional Scottish recipe originally made to celebrate the harvest, and it can be enjoyed as a teatime treat or a dessert.

SERVES 4

75g/3oz crunchy oat cereal
600ml/1 pint/2½ cups Greek
   (US strained plain) yogurt
250g/9oz/1⅓ cups raspberries
heather honey, to serve

VARIATION
*You can use almost any berries
for this recipe. Strawberries and
blackberries work very well. If you
use strawberries, remove the stalks
and cut them into quarters.*

1 Preheat the grill (broiler) to high. Spread the oat cereal on a baking sheet and place under the hot grill for 3–4 minutes, stirring regularly. Set aside on a plate to cool.

2 When the cereal has cooled completely, fold it into the Greek yogurt, then gently fold in 200g/7oz/generous 1 cup of the raspberries, being careful not to crush them.

3 Spoon the yogurt mixture into four serving glasses or dishes, top with the remaining raspberries and serve immediately. Pass around a dish of heather honey to drizzle over the top for extra sweetness and flavour.

Nutritional information per portion: Energy 276kcal/1152kJ; Protein 12.4g; Carbohydrate 17.2g, of which sugars 11.1g; Fat 19.7g, of which saturates 8.7g; Cholesterol 0mg; Calcium 255mg; Fibre 2.5g; Sodium 122mg.

Orange jelly

You can't beat the silky coolness of jelly on a hot summer's day. Use freshly squeezed orange juice if you have the time and facilities to squeeze it, and serve the dessert in pretty stemmed glasses.

SERVES 4

750ml/1¼ pints/3 cups fresh
orange juice
10 sheets leaf gelatine
50g/2oz/¼ cup sugar
handful of fresh mint leaves, chopped
Limoncello liqueur, for drizzling (optional)

COOK'S TIP
The orange juice should be freshly squeezed if possible. If you can't freshly squeeze your own orange juice, do try and use the best quality, freshly squeezed version you can buy.

1 Put the orange juice in a pan. Soak the gelatine in a small bowl of cold water for 5 minutes or until floppy, then drain, squeeze and add it to the juice.

2 Add the sugar. Stir vigorously over low heat until the sugar has dissolved and the gelatine has melted completely.

3 Pour into a shallow square or rectangular mould. Leave to cool, then chill until firm.

4 Remove the set jelly from the refrigerator, and cut into rough cubes. Arrange in four stemmed glasses, sprinkle with the mint leaves and drizzle with Limoncello, if you like.

Nutritional information per portion: Energy 151kcal/641kJ; Protein 9.5g; Carbohydrate 29.6g, of which sugars 29.6g; Fat 0.2g, of which saturates 0g; Cholesterol 0mg; Calcium 26mg; Fibre 0.2g; Sodium 20mg.

Summer pudding

This stunning dessert is an essential part of the English summer and it is deceptively simple to make. Use a mixture of fresh seasonal soft fruits and a good quality loaf of white bread.

SERVES 4–6

about 8 x 1cm/½ in-thick slices of day-old white bread, with crusts removed

800g/1¾ lb/6–7 cups mixed berries, such as strawberries, raspberries, blackcurrants, redcurrants and blueberries

50g/2oz/¼ cup golden caster (superfine) sugar

lightly whipped double (heavy) cream or thick yogurt, to serve (optional)

1 Trim a slice of bread to fit in the base of a 1.2 litre/2 pint/5 cup bowl, then trim another 5–6 slices to line the sides, making sure it comes above the rim.

2 Place all the fruit in a pan with the sugar. Do not add any water. Cook very gently for 4–5 minutes until the juices begin to run. Leave to cool.

3 Spoon most of the berries, and enough of their juices to moisten the fruit, into the bread-lined bowl. Reserve any remaining juice for serving. Fold over the excess bread, then cover the fruit with the remaining slices, trimming to fit. Place a plate that fits inside the bowl directly on top of the pudding. Weight it down with a 900g/2lb weight or a couple of full food cans. Chill for 8 hours.

4 Run a knife around the pudding and turn out on to a plate. Spoon over the reserved juices and fruit, and serve with cream or yogurt, if you like.

Nutritional information per portion: Energy 192kcal/815kJ; Protein 5.2g; Carbohydrate 43.1g, of which sugars 22.1g; Fat 1g, of which saturates 0g; Cholesterol 0mg; Calcium 82mg; Fibre 2.5g; Sodium 245mg.

Fruit trifle

Everyone's favourite, trifle is a classic dessert. The earliest trifles were creamy confections rather like fools, but in the 18th century the dish took the form that is familiar today, with layers of sponge soaked in wine or sherry, topped with syllabub or whipped cream.

SERVES 6–8

1 x 15–18cm/6–7in plain sponge cake
225g/8oz/³⁄₄ cup raspberry jam
150ml/¹⁄₄ pint/²⁄₃ cup medium or sweet sherry
450g/1lb ripe fruit, such as bananas and
    pears, peeled and sliced
300ml/¹⁄₂ pint/1¹⁄₄ cups whipping cream
toasted flaked (sliced) almonds, to decorate

FOR THE CUSTARD
450ml/³⁄₄ pint/scant 2 cups full cream
    (whole) milk
1 vanilla pod (bean)
3 eggs
25g/1oz/2 tbsp caster (superfine) sugar

1 To make the custard, put the milk into a pan with the vanilla pod, split along its length, and bring almost to the boil. Remove from the heat. Leave to cool a little while you whisk the eggs and sugar together lightly. Discard the vanilla pod and gradually whisk the milk into the egg mixture.

2 Rinse out the pan with cold water and return the mixture to it. (Alternatively, use a double boiler, or a bowl over a pan of boiling water.) Stir over a low heat until thick enough to coat the back of a spoon; do not allow it to boil. Pour the custard into a bowl, cover and set aside while you assemble the trifle.

3 Halve the sponge cake horizontally, spread with the raspberry jam and sandwich together. Cut into slices and use to line the bottom and lower sides of a large glass serving bowl. Sprinkle the sponge cake with the sherry.

4 Spread the fruit over the sponge in an even layer. Pour the custard on top, cover with clear film (plastic wrap) to prevent a skin forming, and leave to cool and set. Chill until required.

5 To serve, whip the cream and spread it over the custard, then decorate with the almonds.

VARIATION
The sherry could be replaced with fruit juice, whisky or a fruit liqueur.

Nutritional information per portion: Energy 631kcal/2615kJ; Protein 8.4g; Carbohydrate 24.9g, of which sugars 18.4g; Fat 53.1g, of which saturates 28.4g; Cholesterol 258mg; Calcium 155mg; Fibre 1.4g; Sodium 116mg.

Rhubarb fool

Here is a quick and simple dessert from Scotland that makes the most of rhubarb when it is in season. Serve with shortbread and pass around a dish of honey for those with a sweet tooth.

SERVES 4

450g/1lb rhubarb, trimmed
75g/3oz/scant ½ cup soft light
   brown sugar
whipped double (heavy) cream
   and ready-made thick custard
   (see Step 3)

VARIATION

For a low-fat option, substitute natural (plain) yogurt for the cream.

1 Cut the rhubarb into pieces and wash thoroughly. Stew over a low heat with the sugar and just the water clinging to the rhubarb. This takes about 10 minutes. Set aside to cool.

2 Pass the rhubarb through a fine sieve (strainer) so you have a thick purée.

3 Use equal quantities of the purée, the whipped double cream and thick custard. Combine the purée and custard first then fold in the cream. Chill in the refrigerator before serving.

Nutritional information per portion: Energy 439kcal/1828kJ; Protein 4.6g; Carbohydrate 34.1g, of which sugars 31.8g; Fat 31.7g, of which saturates 18.9g; Cholesterol 80mg; Calcium 233mg; Fibre 1.6g; Sodium 74mg.

Gooseberry fool

This quick-to-make dessert never fails to impress. Like the Rhubarb Fool, it looks attractive served in pretty glasses with small crisp biscuits to provide a contrast in texture.

SERVES 4

450g/1lb gooseberries, cut into pieces

125g/4½oz/¼ cup caster (superfine) sugar, or to taste

300ml/½ pint/1¼ cups double (heavy) cream

crisp biscuits (cookies), to serve

VARIATION

Try other stewed fruits, such as apples, prunes or peaches, if you like.

1 Put the gooseberries into a pan with 30ml/2 tbsp water. Cover and cook gently for about 10 minutes until the fruit is soft. Stir in the sugar to taste.

2 Put the fruit into a nylon sieve (strainer) and press through. Leave to cool.

3 Whip the cream until stiff enough to hold soft peaks. Stir in the gooseberry purée without over-mixing (it looks pretty with some streaks).

4 Spoon the mixture into serving glasses and refrigerate until required.

Nutritional information per portion: Energy 517kcal/2147kJ; Protein 2.6g; Carbohydrate 37.3g, of which sugars 37.3g; Fat 40.7g, of which saturates 25.1g; Cholesterol 103mg; Calcium 85mg; Fibre 2.7g; Sodium 21mg

Syllabub

This dish can be traced back to the 17th century, when it is said to have been made by pouring fresh milk, warm from the cow, on to spiced cider or ale, creating a frothy foam.

SERVES 6

1 orange
65g/2½oz/⅓ cup caster (superfine) sugar
60ml/4 tbsp medium dry sherry
300ml/½ pint/1½ cups double
    (heavy) cream
strips of crystallized orange, to decorate
sponge fingers or crisp biscuits
    (cookies), to serve

1 Finely grate 2.5ml/½ tsp rind from the orange, then squeeze out its juice.

2 Put the orange rind and juice, sugar and sherry into a large bowl and stir until the sugar is completely dissolved. Stir in the cream. Whip the mixture until soft peaks form.

3 Spoon the syllabub into six wine glasses and chill in the refrigerator until ready to serve.

4 To serve, decorate the syllabub with strips of crystallized orange and serve with sponge fingers or crisp biscuits.

Nutritional information per portion: Energy 310kcal/1282kJ; Protein 1.1g; Carbohydrate 14.5g, of which sugars 14.5g; Fat 26.9g, of which saturates 16.7g; Cholesterol 69mg; Calcium 41mg; Fibre 0.3g; Sodium 15mg.

COOK'S TIP
Syllabub is lovely spooned over a bowl of fresh soft fruit such as strawberries, apricots, raspberries or blackberries.

Lemon mousse

Light and airy, this heavenly dessert is also easy to make and refreshing. It strikes a perfect balance between tart citrus flavours and luxuriously rich creaminess.

SERVES 6–8

150ml/2fl oz/¼ cup apple juice

30ml/2 tbsp powdered gelatine

15ml/1 tbsp grated lemon rind, plus extra
   shreds to decorate

90ml/6 tbsp fresh lemon juice

4 eggs, separated

175g/6oz icing (confectioners') sugar

250ml/8fl oz/1 cup double (heavy) cream

VARIATION
*Crumble macaroons into the bottom of
dessert glasses before adding the mousse.*

1 Put the apple juice and gelatine in a bowl and leave until softened. Add 120ml/4fl oz/½ cup boiling water and stir to dissolve the gelatine, then stir in the lemon rind and juice.

2 Combine the egg yolks with 150g/5oz/1¼ cups of the icing sugar in a bowl, and beat until frothy. Fold the gelatine mixture into the egg yolks. Chill for 1 hour.

3 Beat the egg whites until stiff and fold them into the egg yolk mixture.

4 Beat the cream until stiff peaks form, and stir in the remaining icing sugar. Fold half the cream into the egg and lemon mixture.

5 Spoon the mousse into glasses. Chill until set. Serve, decorated with the remaining cream and lemon rind.

Nutritional information per portion: Energy 278kcal/1159kJ; Protein 3.7g; Carbohydrate 23.4g, of which sugars 23.4g; Fat 19.6g, of which saturates 11.2g; Cholesterol 138mg; Calcium 41mg; Fibre 0g; Sodium 43mg.

Belgian chocolate mousse

Belgium is famous around the world for the quality of its chocolate and this mousse is a classic recipe. Be sure to use good quality chocolate for the best results.

SERVES 4

150g/5oz dark (bittersweet) Belgian chocolate, cut into small pieces
200ml/7fl oz/scant 1 cup whipping or double (heavy) cream
75g/3oz/6 tbsp caster (superfine) sugar
2 eggs, separated, at room temperature
chocolate curls or sprinkles, roasted almond slivers, strips of candied orange peel, cocoa powder or extra whipped cream, to decorate (optional)

1 Melt the chocolate in a heatproof bowl over a pan of simmering water. Leave to cool to room temperature.

2 In a clean bowl, whip the cream with 12g/¹/₂ oz/1 tbsp of the sugar until it forms soft peaks. Set aside.

3 In a grease-free, bowl, whisk the egg whites, gradually adding 50g/2oz/ 4 tbsp of the sugar, until stiff.

4 Whisk the egg yolks in a third bowl, gradually adding the last of the sugar, until foamy. Fold into the chocolate.

5 Using a spatula, carefully fold in the whipped cream, then the egg whites.

6 Spoon or pipe into ramekins or dessert glasses and leave to set for at least 4 hours. Serve plain or with any of the suggested decorations.

Nutritional information per portion: Energy 550kcal/2290kJ; Protein 5.9g; Carbohydrate 44.3g, of which sugars 43.9g; Fat 40.1g, of which saturates 23.8g; Cholesterol 166mg; Calcium 61mg; Fibre 1g; Sodium 50mg.

Strawberry mousse

This rich and luxurious mousse is a real treat that will be enjoyed by adults and children alike, and is a great recipe for when there is a glut of strawberries in the summer.

SERVES 4

500g/1¼ lb/5–6 cups strawberries
100g/3½ oz/scant 1 cup icing
   (confectioners') sugar
400ml/14fl oz/1⅔ cups double
   (heavy) cream
25g/1oz/¼ cup flaked (sliced) almonds

COOK'S TIP

For best results, use freshly picked strawberries. Rinse them lightly, if necessary, but do not soak in water or they will become soggy and lose flavour. Pat dry with kitchen paper.

1 Cut half of the strawberries into quarters. Place them in a single layer in a decorative glass bowl. Sprinkle half of the icing sugar on top.

2 In a food processor or blender, purée the remaining strawberries with half of the cream. Add 30–60ml/ 2–4 tbsp of the remaining icing sugar, depending on taste, and process until smooth. Pour over the cut strawberries in the bowl.

3 Toast the almonds over medium heat in a dry frying pan until golden, shaking the pan often to prevent them from burning. Leave to cool.

4 Beat the remaining cream with enough of the remaining icing sugar to sweeten it. Spread or pipe the cream over the purée. Sprinkle the toasted almonds on top, cover with clear film (plastic wrap) and place in the refrigerator until ready to serve.

Nutritional information per portion: Energy 444kcal/1841kJ; Protein 2.7g; Carbohydrate 23.8g, of which sugars 23.7g; Fat 38.2g, of which saturates 22.5g; Cholesterol 91mg; Calcium 65mg; Fibre 1.2g; Sodium 21mg.

Chilled chocolate and espresso mousse

Heady, aromatic espresso coffee adds a distinctive flavour to this smooth, rich mousse. Serve it in stylish chocolate cups for a grown-up dessert on a special occasion.

SERVES 4

225g/8oz plain (semisweet) chocolate
45ml/3 tbsp brewed espresso
25g/1oz/2 tbsp unsalted butter
4 eggs, separated

FOR THE CHOCOLATE CUPS

225g/8oz plain (semisweet) chocolate

COOK'S TIPS

• *For extra indulgence, serve with scoops of mascarpone or clotted cream*
• *Sprinkle with some chopped fresh mint to create an attractive dessert for a dinner party finale.*
• *Omit the espresso if serving this to children who may dislike the coffee taste.*

1 For each chocolate cup, cut a double-thickness 15cm/6in square of foil. Mould it around a small orange, leaving the edges and corners loose to make a cup shape. Remove the orange and press the bottom of the foil case gently on a surface to make a flat base. Repeat to make four foil cups.

2 Break the chocolate into pieces and place in a bowl set over a pan of simmering water. Stir occasionally until the chocolate has melted. Spoon the chocolate into the foil cups, spreading it up the sides with the back of a spoon to give a ragged edge. Chill for 30 minutes or until set. Gently peel away the foil.

3 To make the mousse, put the chocolate and espresso into a bowl set over a pan of simmering water and melt. Add the butter, a little at a time. Remove from the heat and stir in the egg yolks. Whisk the egg whites in a bowl until stiff, then fold into the chocolate mixture. Pour into a bowl and chill for at least 3 hours. To serve, scoop the mousse into the chocolate cups.

Nutritional information per portion: Energy 694kcal/2901kJ; Protein 11.9g; Carbohydrate 71.5g, of which sugars 70.5g; Fat 42.2g, of which saturates 23.7g; Cholesterol 210mg; Calcium 67mg; Fibre 2.8g; Sodium 115mg.

Tiramisù

The name of this classic dessert translates as 'pick me up', which is said to derive from the fact that it is so good, it literally makes you swoon when you eat it.

SERVES 4

225g/8oz/1 cup mascarpone

25g/1oz/¼ cup icing (confectioners')
   sugar, sifted

150ml/¼ pint/²⁄₃ cup strong brewed
   coffee, chilled

300ml/½ pint/1¼ cups double
   (heavy) cream

45ml/3 tbsp coffee liqueur such as
   Tia Maria, Kahlúa or Toussaint

115g/4oz Savoiardi (sponge finger) biscuits

50g/2oz dark (bittersweet) or
   plain (semisweet) chocolate,
   coarsely grated

unsweetened cocoa powder, for dusting

1 Grease and line a 900g/2lb loaf tin (pan) with clear film (plastic wrap). Beat the mascarpone and icing sugar in a bowl. Mix in 30ml/2 tbsp of the coffee. Whip the cream with 15ml/1 tbsp of the liqueur to form soft peaks. Fold it into the mascarpone mixture. Spoon half into the loaf tin and smooth the top.

2 Put the remaining coffee and liqueur in a shallow dish just wider than the Savoiardi biscuits. Using half the biscuits, dip one side of each biscuit into the coffee mixture, then arrange on top of the mascarpone mixture in a layer.

3 Spoon the rest of the mascarpone mixture over and smooth the top. Dip the remaining biscuits in the coffee mixture, and arrange on top. Drizzle any remaining coffee mixture on top. Cover with clear film and chill for 4 hours.

4 Turn out the tiramisù and sprinkle with grated chocolate and cocoa powder.

Nutritional information per portion: Energy 215kcal/894kJ; Protein 8.5g; Carbohydrate 12.4g, of which sugars 10.2g; Fat 13.3g, of which saturates 5.9g; Cholesterol 118mg; Calcium 22mg; Fibre 0.1g; Sodium 48mg.

Panna cotta

This delicious Italian speciality is gaining in popularity and fame all over the world. You can make it completely plain, or add crushed amaretti or coffee, chocolate, citrus rind or liqueur.

SERVES 8

1 litre/1¾ pints/4 cups single
(light) cream
120ml/4fl oz/½ cup icing
(confectioners') sugar
4 sheets gelatine
flavouring: grated rind of 1 lemon, or
1 small cup espresso coffee (about
30ml/2 tbsp very strong black coffee),
or 45ml/3 tbsp liqueur or brandy, or
10ml/2 tsp vanilla extract
60ml/4 tbsp granulated (white) or caster
(superfine) sugar
ground coffee beans, lemon rind, or fruit
coulis, to decorate (optional)

1 Divide the cream into two halves and put into two separate pans. Bring the cream in both pans to just under the boil. To one pan of cream add the icing sugar, and to the other add the gelatine.

2 Whisk both halves constantly until the sugar and gelatine have completely dissolved and the cream is very hot but not boiling. Pour the cream from both pans into one bowl and whisk together. Add the flavouring of your choice (if using) and stir. Cool completely.

3 While the mixture is cooling, put the granulated or caster sugar into a small pan and melt over a low heat, without stirring, until caramelized. Coat the base of eight small metal moulds or ramekins with the caramel. Allow to cool.

4 Strain the panna cotta into the moulds and chill until set. To serve, dip the moulds briefly into hot water and turn out on to plates. Decorate, if you like.

Nutritional information per portion: Energy 134kcal/563kJ; Protein 3g; Carbohydrate 17g, of which sugars 17g; Fat 5g, of which saturates 2g; Cholesterol 202mg; Calcium 27mg; Fibre 0g; Sodium 12mg.

Zabaglione

This is a true labour of love, a combination of fresh egg yolks, marsala wine and sugar, beaten into a frothy mousse-like texture that is just warm. This is a really light and perfect dessert.

SERVES 4

4 egg yolks
60ml/4 tbsp dessert wine, Marsala
   or sweet sherry
60ml/4 tbsp caster (superfine) sugar
amaretti or thin slices of panettone,
   to serve

1 Mix all the ingredients together in a large, rounded, heatproof bowl. Put the bowl over a pan of very hot, but not boiling, water and whisk constantly with an electric whisk until foaming, pale yellow, thick and shiny. This will take up to 10 minutes, or 20 minutes if you use a hand-held balloon whisk.

2 Pour the mixture into glasses and serve with amaretti or thin slices of panettone.

Nutritional information per portion: Energy 134kcal/563kJ; Protein 3g; Carbohydrate 17g, of which sugars 17g; Fat 5g, of which saturates 2g; Cholesterol 202mg; Calcium 27mg; Fibre 0g; Sodium 12mg.

Pashka

This fresh cheese and dried fruit dessert from Russia is made by mixing the ingredients together, putting them in a lined mould and letting all the liquid drain away, creating a firm, dome-shaped pudding. The traditional mould is conical, but a coffee filter-holder or a clean plastic flower pot work equally well. Paskha needs to be made a few days in advance.

SERVES 6–8

500g/1¼ lb/2½ cups ricotta cheese or
   cottage cheese
75g/3oz/6 tbsp unsalted butter, softened
275g/10oz/1½ cups caster (superfine) sugar
30ml/2 tbsp vanilla sugar
150ml/¼ pint/⅔ cup whipping cream

30ml/2 tbsp smetana or crème fraîche
2 egg yolks
40g/1½ oz/generous ¼ cup raisins
grated rind of 1 lemon
glacé (candied) orange or lemon rind and
   blanched almonds, to decorate

1 If using cottage cheese, first push the cheese through a sieve (strainer). Put the ricotta or cottage cheese in a sieve and stand the sieve over a bowl. Leave to drain overnight in a cold place.

2 Line a clean 750ml/1¼ pint/3 cup coffee filter, or a flower pot with a drainage hole, with damp muslin (cheesecloth), allowing the edges of the muslin to overhang the edges.

3 Transfer the drained cheese into a mixing bowl, add the butter, caster sugar and vanilla sugar, and beat together until smooth.

4 Pour the whipping cream into a separate bowl and whisk until it forms soft peaks. Stir the cream, smetana or crème fraîche and egg yolks into the cheese mixture then whisk until fluffy and smooth. Add the raisins and grated lemon rind and stir together.

5 Spoon the mixture into the lined coffee filter or flower pot and fold the edges of the muslin into the centre. Cover with a small saucer that fits inside the container and put a 500g/1¼ lb weight on top. Stand in a bowl or soup plate and leave in a cold place, to drain, for one to three days.

6 Remove the weight and saucer. Unfold the muslin and very carefully turn the paskha out on to a serving plate. Gently remove the muslin. Serve the paskha decorated with candied fruits and blanched almonds.

Nutritional information per portion: Energy 369kcal/1544kJ; Protein 9.3g; Carbohydrate 41.9g, of which sugars 41.9g; Fat 19.1g, of which saturates 11.5g; Cholesterol 100mg; Calcium 118mg; Fibre 0.1g; Sodium 256mg.

Crème brûlée

This pudding is thought to have originated in England in the 18th century. The soft and creamy egg custard is flavoured with vanilla and topped with a brittle caramelized sugar crust.

SERVES 6

1 vanilla pod (bean)
1 litre/1¾ pints/4 cups double
    (heavy) cream
6 egg yolks
90g/3½ oz/½ cup caster
    (superfine) sugar
30ml/2 tbsp almond or orange
    liqueur (optional)
75g/3oz/⅓ cup soft light brown sugar

COOK'S TIP

It is best to make the custards the day before you wish to eat them, so that they can become really cold and firm.

1 Preheat the oven to 150°C/300°F/Gas 2. Place six 125ml/4fl oz/½ cup ramekins in an ovenproof dish and set aside. Split the vanilla pod and scrape the seeds into a pan. Add the cream and bring just to the boil, stirring frequently. Remove from the heat and cover. Set aside for 15–20 minutes.

2 Whisk the egg yolks, caster sugar and liqueur, if using, until blended. Whisk in the hot cream and strain into a large jug (pitcher). Divide among the ramekins.

3 Pour enough boiling water into the dish to come about halfway up the sides of the ramekins. Cover with foil and bake for 30 minutes until just set. Push a knife into the centre – if it comes out clean the custards are cooked. Remove the ramekins from the dish and leave to cool. Return to the dry dish and chill.

4 Preheat the grill (broiler). Sprinkle the brown sugar over the custards and grill (broil) for 30–60 seconds until the sugar caramelizes. Chill until set.

Nutritional information per portion: Energy 996kcal/4116kJ; Protein 5.7g; Carbohydrate 31.6g, of which sugars 31.6g; Fat 95g, of which saturates 57.2g; Cholesterol 430mg; Calcium 120mg; Fibre 0g; Sodium 47mg.

Crème caramel

Baked caramel custards have long been enjoyed throughout Europe, and each nation has its own twist on the recipe. Serve this classic French version as it is, or with cream.

SERVES 6

75g/3oz/scant ½ cup granulated
   (white) sugar
600ml/1 pint/2½ cups milk
1 vanilla pod (bean) or a few drops
   of vanilla extract
6 eggs
75g/3oz/scant ½ cup caster
   (superfine) sugar

COOK'S TIPS
• To loosen the custards before turning them out on to serving plates, run a knife around the edge and tilt the dish to ease the custard away from the sides.
• You can also use this mixture to make one large Crème Caramel. Put the mixture in a 900ml/1½ pint/3¾ cup baking dish and bake for 1–1½ hours, until set.

1 Preheat the oven to 160°C/325°F/Gas 3. Put the granulated sugar into a heavy pan and stir over medium heat to make a golden caramel syrup. Remove from the heat and carefully stir in 15ml/1 tbsp water.

2 Divide the caramel among six warmed ramekins. Using oven gloves, tilt the ramekins to coat the bases with the hot caramel, then place in a roasting pan.

3 To make the custard, scald the milk in a small pan with the vanilla pod, if using. Lightly beat the eggs and caster sugar in a bowl and, when the milk is nearly boiling, remove the vanilla pod and whisk in the egg and sugar mixture. Add the vanilla extract, if using. Pour the custard into the ramekins.

4 Fill the roasting pan to a depth of about 2.5cm/1in with cold water, cover the ramekins with buttered baking parchment and bake in the centre of the oven until the custard has set, about 30 minutes. Cool, then chill.

5 Turn the ramekins out on to small plates and serve (see Cook's Tips).

Nutritional information per portion 233kcal/983kJ; Protein 11g; Carbohydrate 30.8g, of which sugars 30.8g; Fat 8.4g, of which saturates 2.9g; Cholesterol 234mg; Calcium 168mg; Fibre 0g; Sodium 129mg.

Floating islands

The French name for this dish is Oeufs à la Neige, meaning snow eggs. Traditionally the meringues are poached in milk, which is then used to make the rich custard sauce. However, this method uses water for poaching, which gives a much lighter result.

SERVES 4–6

1 vanilla pod (bean)
600ml/1 pint/2½ cups milk
8 egg yolks
50g/2oz/¼ cup granulated (white) sugar

FOR THE MERINGUES

4 egg whites
1.5ml/¼ tsp cream of tartar
225g/8oz/1¼ cups caster (superfine) sugar

FOR THE CARAMEL

150g/5oz/¾ cup granulated (white) sugar

1 Using a knife with a sharp point, carefully split the vanilla pod lengthways. Scrape the black seeds into a pan and add the pod. Add the milk and bring to the boil over a medium-high heat, stirring frequently. Remove the pan from the heat and cover with a lid. Set aside for 15–20 minutes to cool slightly.

2 In a large bowl, whisk the egg yolks and sugar for 2–3 minutes until thick and creamy. Remove and discard the vanilla pod from the hot milk, then whisk the milk into the egg mixture and return to the pan.

3 With a wooden spoon, stir the sauce over medium-low heat until it begins to thicken and coats the back of the spoon; do not allow the custard to boil.

4 Strain into a chilled bowl, allow to cool, stirring occasionally, then chill until ready to serve.

5 Half-fill a large frying pan or wide shallow pan with water and bring just to simmering point. In a clean grease-free bowl, whisk the egg whites slowly until they are frothy. Add the cream of tartar, increase the speed and continue whisking until they form soft peaks. Gradually sprinkle over the caster sugar, about 30ml/2 tbsp at a time, and whisk until the whites are stiff and glossy.

6 Using two tablespoons, form egg-shaped meringues and slide them into the water – you may need to work in batches. Poach them for 2–3 minutes, turning once, until the meringue is just firm. Use a slotted spoon to transfer the meringues from the pan to a baking sheet lined with kitchen paper to drain.

7 Divide the cold custard between shallow serving dishes or plates and arrange the meringues on top.

8 To make the caramel, put the sugar into a small pan with 45ml/3 tbsp of water. Bring to the boil over a high heat, carefully swirling the pan to dissolve the sugar. Do not allow to boil until it is completely dissolved, then boil, without stirring, until the syrup turns a dark caramel colour.

9 Working quickly before it hardens, drizzle the caramel over the poached meringues and custard in a zigzag pattern. Serve cold.

COOK'S TIP
If you do not have a vanilla pod (bean), you can use 5ml/1 tsp vanilla extract instead.

Nutritional information per portion: Energy 414kcal/1755kJ; Protein 9.5g; Carbohydrate 78.7g, of which sugars 78.7g; Fat 9g, of which saturates 3.2g; Cholesterol 275mg; Calcium 190mg; Fibre 0g; Sodium 100mg.

Meringues with chestnut cream

This dessert takes its name, Petits Monts Blancs, from the famous peak in the French Alps, Mont Blanc, as the meringues, piled high with chestnut purée and whipped cream, resemble it.

SERVES 6

2 egg whites
pinch of cream of tartar
100g/3½oz/½ cup caster (superfine) sugar
2.5ml/½ tsp vanilla extract
chocolate shavings, to decorate

FOR THE CHESTNUT CREAM
60g/2oz/⅓ cup caster (superfine) sugar
125ml/4fl oz/½ cup water

450g/1lb can unsweetened chestnut purée
5ml/1 tsp vanilla extract
350ml/12fl oz/1½ cups double (heavy) cream

FOR THE CHOCOLATE SAUCE
225g/8oz plain (semisweet)
  chocolate, chopped
175g/6oz/¾ cup whipping cream
30ml/2 tbsp rum or brandy (optional)

1 Preheat the oven to 140°C/275°F/Gas 1. Line a baking sheet with baking parchment. Use a small plate to outline six 9cm/3½in circles with a pencil and turn the paper over (so the meringue does not touch the pencil marks).

2 In a clean grease-free bowl, using an electric mixer, beat the egg whites slowly until frothy. Add the cream of tartar, then increase the speed and continue beating until they form soft peaks. Gradually sprinkle over the sugar, 30ml/2 tbsp at a time, and continue beating until the whites are stiff and glossy. Beat in the vanilla extract.

3 Spoon the whisked egg whites into a large piping (pastry) bag fitted with a medium-size plain or star nozzle and pipe six spirals following the outlines on the marked paper. Bake for about 1 hour until the meringues feel firm and crisp, lowering the oven temperature if they begin to brown. Using a thin metal spatula, transfer the meringues to a wire rack to cool completely.

4 To make the chestnut cream, place the sugar and water in a small pan over a medium-high heat and bring to the boil, stirring until the sugar dissolves. Boil for about 5 minutes, then remove the pan from the heat and set aside to cool. Put the chestnut purée in a food processor fitted with the metal blade and process until smooth. With the machine running, slowly add the sugar syrup in a thin stream until the chestnut purée is soft, but still holds its shape (you may not need all the syrup). Add the vanilla extract and process again, then spoon into a medium bowl.

5 In another bowl, with an electric mixer, whisk the cream until soft peaks form, then add a tablespoonful to the chestnut cream and pulse to combine. Chill the remaining whipped cream.

6 Spoon the chestnut cream into a piping bag fitted with a large star nozzle. Pipe a mound of chestnut cream in a swirl on to each meringue, then pipe or spoon the remaining cream on top of the chestnut cream to resemble a mountain peak. Chill until ready to serve.

7 To make the chocolate sauce, heat the chocolate and cream in a small pan over a medium-low heat, stirring frequently. Remove the pan from the heat and stir in the rum or brandy, if using. Set aside to cool, stirring occasionally. (Do not chill or the sauce will set.)

8 To serve, place each meringue on a plate and arrange the chocolate shavings on top. Serve the chocolate sauce separately.

Nutritional information per portion: Energy 735kcal/3055kJ; Protein 6g; Carbohydrate 57g, of which sugars 40g; Fat 55g, of which saturates 33g; Cholesterol 113; Calcium 86mg; Fibre 3.3g; Sodium 50mg.

Pies, tarts and cheesecakes

Making your own pastry is a great way to impress your guests, especially when you add delectable fillings, such as blueberries, plums, almonds or pumpkin. Whether it's for a hearty deep-dish pie or an elegant fruit tart, homemade pastry is divine. This chapter also contains rich, indulgent cheesecakes, such as Raspberry, Mascarpone and White Chocolate Cheesecake, which are sure to provide a satisfying end to any meal.

Deep-dish apple pie

This all-time classic favourite is made with rich shortcrust pastry. Inside, sugar, spices and flour create a deliciously thick and syrupy sauce with the apple juices.

SERVES 6

115g/4oz/1/2 cup caster (superfine) sugar
45ml/3 tbsp plain (all-purpose) flour
2.5ml/1/2 tsp ground cinnamon
finely grated rind of 1 orange
900g/2lb cooking apples
1 egg white, lightly beaten
30ml/2 tbsp demerara (raw) sugar
whipped cream, to serve

FOR THE PASTRY

350g/12oz/3 cups plain (all-purpose) flour
a pinch of salt
175g/6oz/3/4 cup butter, diced
about 75ml/5 tbsp chilled water

1 To make the pastry, sift the flour and salt into a bowl and rub in the butter. Sprinkle over the water and mix to a firm, soft dough. Knead lightly until smooth. Wrap in clear film (plastic wrap) and chill for 30 minutes.

2 Combine the caster sugar, flour, cinnamon and orange rind in a bowl. Peel, core and thinly slice the apples. Add to the sugar mixture, then toss gently.

3 Put a baking sheet in the oven and preheat to 200°C/400°F/Gas 6. Roll out just over half the pastry and use to line a 23cm/9in pie dish that is 4cm/11/2in deep. Allow the edges to overhang slightly. Spoon in the filling, doming it in the centre.

4 Roll out the remaining pastry to form the lid. Lightly brush the edges with a little water, then place the lid over the apple filling. Trim the pastry with a sharp knife. Gently press the edges together to seal, then knock up the edge with the back of a knife. Re-roll the pastry trimmings and cut out apple and leaf shapes. Brush the top of the pie with egg white. Arrange the pastry apples and leaves on top.

5 Brush again with egg white, then sprinkle with demerara sugar. Make two small slits in the top of the pie to allow steam to escape.

6 Bake for 30 minutes, then lower the oven temperature to 180°C/350°F/Gas 4 and bake for a further 15 minutes until the pastry is golden and the apples are soft – check by inserting a small sharp knife or skewer through one of the slits in the top of the pie. Serve hot, with some whipped cream.

Nutritional information per portion: Energy 591kcal/2488kJ; Protein 7.4g; Carbohydrate 89.9g, of which sugars 39.8g; Fat 25g, of which saturates 15.3g; Cholesterol 62mg; Calcium 117mg; Fibre 4.4g; Sodium 193mg.

Plum pie

English fruit pies are made either in a pie dish with a deep filling, as here, or on a plate with a crust both top and bottom. Serve the pie with whipped cream or custard.

SERVES 6

200g/7oz/1¾ cups plain
   (all-purpose) flour
25g/1oz/4 tbsp icing (confectioners') sugar
115g/4oz/½ cup butter, diced
1 egg, lightly beaten
800g/1¾ lb plums, stoned (pitted)
about 75g/3oz caster (superfine) sugar,
   plus extra for sprinkling
beaten egg white, to glaze

COOK'S TIP

Check the pie is cooked by inserting a knife through the slit in the pastry – the plums should be soft.

1 Sift the flour and icing sugar into a bowl. Rub in the butter. Stir in the egg and gather together into a smooth dough. Chill for 30 minutes.

2 Preheat the oven to 190°C/375°F/Gas 5. Place half the plums in a 1 litre/1¾ pint/4 cup pie dish. Sprinkle the caster sugar over them, adjusting the amount according to the sweetness of the fruit. Add the remaining plums.

3 Roll out the pastry on a floured surface to a shape slightly larger than the dish. Dampen the edges of the dish with a little egg white and cover with the pastry. Trim and pinch the edges to make a decorative edging. Brush the top with egg white and sprinkle with caster sugar. Make a small slit in the centre.

4 Cook for 35–40 minutes until the pastry is golden brown (see Cook's Tip).

Nutritional information per portion: Energy 360kcal/1516kJ; Protein 4.1g; Carbohydrate 57g, of which sugars 25.5g; Fat 14.5g, of which saturates 7.5g; Cholesterol 26mg; Calcium 73mg; Fibre 2.9g; Sodium 61mg.

Mango pie

This recipe comes straight from the Caribbean and captures all the sunshine flavours of that exotic locale. For the tastiest pie, make sure the mangoes are ripe. Serve with cream or ice cream.

SERVES 6

175g/6oz/1½ cups plain
  (all-purpose) flour
a pinch of salt
75g/3oz/⅓ cup unsalted butter,
  chilled and diced
25g/1oz/2 tbsp white vegetable fat,
  chilled and diced
15ml/1 tbsp caster (superfine) sugar,
  plus extra for sprinkling
about 45ml/3 tbsp cold water
beaten egg, to glaze
cream or ice cream, to serve

FOR THE FILLING

2 mangoes, peeled, 1 chopped and 1 sliced
45ml/3 tbsp fresh lime juice
115g/4oz/½ cup caster (superfine) sugar
15ml/1 tbsp arrowroot mixed to a paste
  with 15ml/1 tbsp water

1 Sift the flour and salt into a large bowl. Rub in the butter and white vegetable fat, then add the caster sugar. Add enough water to make a dough. Knead lightly, then roll out two-thirds of the pastry. Use to line an 18cm/7in pie dish. Wrap the rest in clear film (plastic wrap). Chill the pastry and pastry case for 30 minutes.

2 Meanwhile, make the filling. Place the chopped mango in a pan with the lime juice and caster sugar. Cover and cook for 10 minutes or until soft. Add the arrowroot paste and cook, stirring constantly, until thickened. Set aside to cool.

3 Preheat the oven to 190°C/375°F/Gas 5. Pour the mango sauce into the pastry case and top with the mango slices. Roll out the remaining pastry to make a lid. Dampen the rim of the pastry case and add the pastry lid. Crimp the edges to seal, then cut a cross in the centre to allow the steam to escape.

4 Glaze with the beaten egg and sprinkle with sugar. Bake for 35–40 minutes, until golden. Cool slightly, then serve warm with cream or ice cream.

Nutritional information per portion: Energy 276kcal/1152kJ; Protein 12.4g; Carbohydrate 17.2g, of which sugars 11.1g; Fat 19.7g, of which saturates 8.7g; Cholesterol 0mg; Calcium 255mg; Fibre 2.5g; Sodium 122mg.

Peach leaf pie

Juicy, lightly spiced peach slices are covered with a decorative crust made entirely from individual pastry leaves to make this spectacular pie.

SERVES 8

1.2kg/2¹/₂ lb ripe peaches

juice of 1 lemon

115g/4oz/¹/₂ cup sugar

45ml/3 tbsp cornflour (cornstarch)

1.5ml/¹/₄ tsp freshly grated nutmeg

2.5ml/¹/₂ tsp ground cinnamon

25g/1oz/2 tbsp butter, diced

1 egg, beaten with 45ml/1 tbsp water,
    to glaze

FOR THE PASTRY

225g/8oz/2 cups plain (all-purpose) flour

4ml/³/₄ tsp salt

115g/4oz/¹/₂ cup cold butter, diced

40g/1¹/₂ oz/3 tbsp white vegetable
    fat, diced

75–90ml/5–6 tbsp chilled water

1 To make the pastry, sift the flour and salt into a bowl. Rub in the butter and fat. Sprinkle over just enough of the water to bind the dry ingredients, and use a fork to bring it together to form a soft dough. Gather into two balls, one slightly larger than the other. Wrap each in clear film (plastic wrap). Chill for 30 minutes. Put a baking sheet in the oven and preheat to 220°C/425°F/Gas 7.

2 Drop a few peaches at a time into a pan of boiling water, leave for 20 seconds, then transfer to a bowl of cold water. When cool, peel and slice, then mix with the lemon juice, sugar, cornflour and spices. Set aside.

3 Roll out the larger piece of pastry to 3mm/¹/₈in thick. Line a 23cm/9in pie plate and chill. Roll out the other piece and cut out enough 7.5cm/3in long leaf shapes to cover the pie. Mark on veins with a knife. Brush the base with egg glaze. Add the peaches, piling to a dome in the centre. Dot with butter.

4 Make a ring of leaves around the outside, attaching them with a dab of egg glaze. Place another ring of leaves above. Continue until the pie is covered. Brush with egg glaze. Bake on the hot baking sheet for 10 minutes. Lower the oven to 180°C/350°F/Gas 4 and continue to bake for 35–40 minutes until golden.

Nutritional information per portion: Energy 390kcal/1638kJ; Protein 4.4g; Carbohydrate 53.8g of which sugars 27.2g; Fat 19g, of which saturates 10.7g; Cholesterol 52mg; Calcium 62mg; Fibre 3.2g; Sodium 152mg.

Shoofly pie

An unsweetened pastry case made with a simple combination of butter and cream cheese complements the wonderful dark sweet filling of this pie from the American Deep South.

SERVES 8

115g/4oz/1 cup plain (all-purpose) flour
115g/4oz/½ cup firmly packed soft dark brown sugar
1.5ml/¼ tsp each salt, ground ginger, cinnamon, mace and grated nutmeg
75g/3oz/6 tbsp cold butter, diced
2 eggs
185g/6½ oz/½ cup black treacle (molasses)
120ml/4fl oz/½ cup boiling water
2.5ml/½ tsp bicarbonate of soda (baking soda)

FOR THE PASTRY

115g/4oz/½ cup cream cheese
115g/4oz/½ cup butter, diced
115g/4oz/1 cup plain (all-purpose) flour

1 To make the pastry, put the cream cheese and butter in a mixing bowl. Sift over the flour, and rub in to bind the dough. Wrap in clear film (plastic wrap). Chill for at least 30 minutes.

2 Preheat the oven to 190°C/375°F/ Gas 5. Mix the flour, brown sugar, salt, spices and butter in a bowl. Rub in with your fingertips until it resembles coarse breadcrumbs, then set aside.

3 Roll out the pastry to a thickness of 3mm/⅛in and use to line a 23cm/ 9in pie plate. Trim and flute the edges.

4 Spoon one-third of the filling mixture into the pastry case. Whisk the eggs with the treacle in a large bowl. Put a baking sheet in the oven.

5 Pour the boiling water into a bowl and stir in the bicarbonate of soda; it will foam. Add immediately to the egg mixture and whisk. Pour into the pastry case and sprinkle the remaining filling mixture over evenly.

6 Place on the hot baking sheet and bake for 35 minutes, or until browned. Cool, then serve at room temperature.

Nutritional information per portion: Energy 472kcal/1975kJ; Protein 5.2g; Carbohydrate 53g, of which sugars 31g; Fat 28.1g, of which saturates 17.1g; Cholesterol 112mg; Calcium 201mg; Fibre 0.9g; Sodium 248mg.

Blueberry pie

American blueberries or European bilberries can be used for this pie. You may need to add a little more sugar if you are lucky enough to find native bilberries.

SERVES 6

800g/1¾ lb/7 cups blueberries
75g/3oz/6 tbsp caster (superfine) sugar,
   plus extra for sprinkling
45ml/3 tbsp cornflour (cornstarch)
grated rind and juice of ½ orange
grated rind of ½ lemon
2.5ml/½ tsp ground cinnamon
15g/½ oz/1 tbsp butter, diced
1 egg, beaten
whipped cream, to serve

FOR THE PASTRY

275g/10oz/2½ cups plain
   (all-purpose) flour
a pinch of salt
75g/3oz/6 tbsp butter, diced
50g/2oz/¼ cup white vegetable
   fat, diced
60–75ml/4–5 tbsp chilled water

1 To make the pastry, sift the flour and salt into a bowl and rub in the fat. Sprinkle over most of the water and mix to a soft dough. Add more water if necessary. Knead lightly. Wrap in clear film (plastic wrap) and chill. Preheat the oven to 200°C/400°F/Gas 6. Roll out half the pastry and use to line a 23cm/9in pie dish, allowing the excess pastry to overhang the edge.

2 In a bowl, mix the blueberries, caster sugar, cornflour, orange rind and juice, lemon rind and cinnamon. Spoon into the pastry case and dot with butter.

3 Roll out the remaining pastry to make a lid for the pie. Trim off the excess, leaving a rim all round. Cut the rim at 2.5cm/1in intervals, then fold each pastry section over on itself to form a triangle. Re-roll the trimmings and cut out pastry decorations. Attach them to the pastry lid with a little beaten egg.

4 Glaze the pastry with the beaten egg and sprinkle with caster sugar. Bake for 30 minutes, or until golden. Serve warm or cold with whipped cream.

Nutritional information per portion: Energy 458kcal/1915kJ; Protein 4.7g; Carbohydrate 60g, of which sugars 20.4g; Fat 23.8g, of which saturates 1.3g; Cholesterol 5mg; Calcium 95mg; Fibre 5.6g; Sodium 143mg.

Linzertorte

Use a good quality jam or conserve to fill the cinnamon and almond pastry case in this traditional Austrian speciality, and dust it with icing sugar before serving.

SERVES 8–10

225g/8oz/³/4 cup raspberry jam
1 egg yolk
icing (confectioners') sugar, for dusting
custard, to serve (optional)

FOR THE PASTRY
200g/7oz/scant 1 cup butter
200g/7oz/scant 1 cup caster
    (superfine) sugar
3 eggs, plus 1 egg yolk
2.5ml/¹/2 tsp ground cinnamon
grated rind of ¹/2 lemon
115g/4oz/2 cups fine sweet biscuit
    (cookie) crumbs
150g/5oz/1¹/4 cups ground almonds
225g/8oz/2 cups plain (all-purpose)
    flour, sifted

1 Preheat the oven to 190°C/375°F/Gas 5. To make the pastry, cream the butter and sugar together until light. Slowly add the eggs and one of the egg yolks, beating all the time, then add the cinnamon and rind. Stir the crumbs and ground almonds into the mixture. Mix well, then add the sifted flour. Knead to form a dough, then wrap in clear film (plastic wrap). Chill for about 30 minutes.

2 Roll out two-thirds of the pastry on a lightly floured surface and use to line a deep 25cm/10in loose-based flan tin (pan). Press the pastry into the sides and trim the edge. Spread the raspberry jam generously and evenly over the base of the pastry case. Roll out the remaining pastry into a long rectangle. Cut the rectangle into even strips with a sharp knife and arrange in a lattice pattern over the jam filling.

3 Lightly beat the remaining egg yolk in a small bowl, then brush it evenly over the pastry rim and lattice. Bake the torte for 45 minutes, until golden brown. Leave to cool in the tin for a few minutes before turning out on to a wire rack. Just before serving, sift a little icing sugar on top. Serve with custard, if you like.

Nutritional information per portion: Energy 537kcal/2247kJ; Protein 8.5g; Carbohydrate 63g, of which sugars 39.1g; Fat 29.7g, of which saturates 12.8g; Cholesterol 125mg; Calcium 106mg; Fibre 2.1g; Sodium 223mg.

Bakewell tart

This is a modern version of a traditional pudding, allegedly first made by accident in Bakewell, in the north of England. The tart has become a universal favourite.

SERVES 4

115g/4oz/1 cup plain
   (all-purpose) flour
a pinch of salt
50g/2oz/4 tbsp butter, diced, plus
   115g/4oz/½ cup butter, melted
20ml/2 tbsp cold water
30ml/2 tbsp raspberry or apricot jam
2 whole eggs and 2 extra yolks
115g/4oz/generous ½ cup caster
   (superfine) sugar
55g/2oz/⅔ cup ground almonds
a few drops of almond extract
icing (confectioners') sugar, to dust

1 Sift the flour and salt, then rub in the diced butter until the mixture resembles fine crumbs. Stir in the water and gather into a smooth ball of dough. Wrap in clear film (plastic wrap). Chill for 30 minutes. Preheat the oven to 200°C/400°F/Gas 6.

2 Roll out the pastry and use to line an 18cm/7in loose-based flan tin (pan). Spread the jam over the pastry.

3 Whisk the eggs, egg yolks and sugar together until thick and pale. Stir in the melted butter, ground almonds and almond extract.

4 Pour the mixture over the jam in the pastry case (pie shell). Cook the tart for 30 minutes until just set and browned. Sift a little icing sugar over the top before serving warm or at room temperature.

Nutritional information per portion: Energy 700kcal/2919kJ; Protein 10.8g; Carbohydrate 57.1g, of which sugars 36.7g; Fat 49.9g, of which saturates 17.1g; Cholesterol 257mg; Calcium 110mg; Fibre 0.9g; Sodium 394mg.

Yorkshire curd tart

The distinguishing characteristic of Yorkshire curd tarts is allspice, or 'clove pepper' as it was known locally. This English tart tastes superb and is not too sweet.

SERVES 8

90g/3½ oz/scant ½ cup soft light
   brown sugar
a large pinch of ground allspice
3 eggs, beaten
grated rind and juice of 1 lemon
40g/1½ oz/3 tbsp butter, melted
450g/1lb/2 cups curd (farmer's) cheese
75g/3oz/scant ½ cup raisins
cream, to serve (optional)

FOR THE PASTRY

225g/8oz/2 cups plain (all-purpose) flour
115g/4oz/½ cup butter, diced
1 egg yolk
15–30ml/1–2 tbsp chilled water

1 To make the pastry, place the flour in a mixing bowl. Rub in the butter. Stir in the egg yolk and add just enough water to bind the mixture together to form a dough.

2 Put the dough on a floured surface, knead lightly and briefly, then form into a ball. Roll out the pastry thinly and use to line a 20cm/8in fluted loose-based flan tin (pan). Cover with clear film (plastic wrap) and chill for 15 minutes.

3 Preheat the oven to 190°C/375°F/ Gas 5. Mix the sugar with the ground allspice in a bowl, then stir in the eggs, lemon rind and juice, butter, curd cheese and raisins. Mix well.

4 Pour the filling into the pastry case, then bake for 40 minutes, or until the pastry is cooked and the filling is lightly set and golden brown. Cut the tart into wedges while it is still slightly warm, and serve with cream, if you like.

Nutritional information per portion: Energy 480kcal/2005kJ; Protein 16.2g; Carbohydrate 48.2g, of which sugars 23.7g; Fat 27g, of which saturates 15.8g; Cholesterol 173mg; Calcium 153mg; Fibre 1.2g; Sodium 451mg.

Walnut and honey tart

This tart has a truly Scottish feel to it, especially if you use heather honey made by bees that feed on wild heather. Serve this tart with plenty of whipped cream.

SERVES 4

90g/3½ oz ready-made sweet
   shortcrust pastry
6 sugar cubes
200g/7oz/1¾ cups walnuts
75ml/5 tbsp good honey
45ml/3 tbsp double (heavy) cream

1 Preheat the oven to 200°C/400°F/Gas 6. Roll the pastry out to a disc measuring about 25cm/10in across and allow to rest for 15 minutes. Place on a baking sheet then bake in the preheated oven for about 15 minutes.

2 Put the sugar and 60ml/4 tbsp water in a pan and heat until it caramelizes, stirring constantly. Add the walnuts and coat with caramel, toasting them lightly in the pan for a few minutes. Remove from the heat and allow to cool slightly.

3 Add the honey and cream, mixing thoroughly until the mixture has cooled completely.

4 Spread the walnut mixture over the pastry disc and rest for 10 minutes before serving.

Nutritional information per portion: Energy 563kcal/2338kJ; Protein 9.1g; Carbohydrate 35.9g, of which sugars 30.8g; Fat 43.5g, of which saturates 6.6g; Cholesterol 15mg; Calcium 70mg; Fibre 2g; Sodium 67mg.

Blackcurrant tart

Blackcurrants are cultivated throughout Europe, and are widely available in North America. This tart makes the most of these exquisite summer fruits, which are rich in vitamin C.

SERVES 4

500g/1¼ lb/5 cups blackcurrants
115g/4oz/generous ½ cup caster
 (superfine) sugar
250g/9oz ready-made puff pastry
50g/2oz/½ cup icing
 (confectioners') sugar
whipped cream, to serve

1 Preheat the oven to 220°C/425°F/Gas 7. Trim the blackcurrants, making sure you remove all the stalks and any hard parts in the middle. Add the caster sugar and mix well.

2 Roll out the pastry to about 3mm/⅛in thick and cut out four discs roughly the size of a side plate or a large cereal bowl. Then, using a smaller plate (or bowl), lightly mark with the point of a knife a circle about 2cm/¾in inside each disc.

3 Spread the blackcurrants over the discs, keeping them within the marked inner circle. Bake in the oven for 15 minutes. Dust generously with the icing sugar before serving. Serve hot with a large dollop of whipped cream, or serve cold as a teatime snack.

Nutritional information per portion: Energy 426kcal/1798kJ; Protein 4.9g; Carbohydrate 73.2g, of which sugars 50.9g; Fat 15.3g, of which saturates 3.8g; Cholesterol 0mg; Calcium 133mg; Fibre 4.5g; Sodium 200mg.

Tarte tatin

This French tart was first made by two sisters who served it in their restaurant near Sologne in the Loire Valley. A special tarte tatin tin is ideal, but an ovenproof frying pan will do very well.

SERVES 8–10

225g/½ lb ready-made puff or
   shortcrust pastry
10–12 large Golden Delicious apples
lemon juice, for sprinkling
120g/4oz/½ cup butter, cut into pieces
120g/4oz/½ cup caster (superfine) sugar
2.5ml/½ tsp ground cinnamon
crème fraîche or whipped cream, to serve

COOK'S TIP

If you do not have a heavy flameproof tarte tatin tin (pan), use a deep, straight-sided frying pan. If the handle is not ovenproof, wrap it well in several layers of strong foil to protect it from the heat.

1 On a floured surface, roll out the pastry into a 28cm/11in round less than 6mm/¼in thick. Transfer to a floured baking sheet and chill. Peel the apples, cut them in half lengthways and core. Sprinkle generously with lemon juice.

2 In a 25cm/10in tarte tatin tin (tart pan), cook the butter, sugar and cinnamon over medium heat until the butter has melted and sugar dissolved, stirring occasionally. Continue cooking for 6–8 minutes, until a medium caramel colour, then remove from the heat. Arrange the apple halves, standing on their edges, in the tin, fitting them in tightly since they shrink during cooking.

3 Return to the heat and simmer over medium heat for 20–25 minutes until the apples are tender and coloured. Remove from the heat and cool slightly.

4 Preheat the oven to 230°C/450°F/Gas 8. Place the pastry on top of the tin and tuck the edges around the apples. Pierce the pastry in two or three places, then bake for 25–30 minutes until golden. Cool in the tin for 10–15 minutes.

5 Run a knife around the edge of the tin, cover with a plate and invert carefully. Lift off the tin and loosen any apples that stick with a metal spatula.

Nutritional information per portion: Energy 228kcal/954kJ; Protein 1.6g; Carbohydrate 23.7g, of which sugars 15.7g; Fat 15g, of which saturates 6g; Cholesterol 25mg; Calcium 23mg; Fibre 1.1g; Sodium 141mg.

Summer berry tart

This tart is best made with fresh berries, but if they are out of season, this tart is equally delicious made with frozen berries that are available all year round.

SERVES 6–8

500g/1¼ lb fresh or frozen mixed berries
200g/7oz/1 cup caster (superfine) sugar
whipped double (heavy) cream, to serve

FOR THE PASTRY
300g/10oz/2½ cups plain
    (all-purpose) flour
115g/4oz/½ cup unsalted butter, diced
50g/2oz/¼ cup caster (superfine) sugar
1 egg, beaten

1 To make the pastry, put the flour in a food processor. Add the butter and then, using a pulsing action, mix together until the mixture resembles fine breadcrumbs. Stir in the sugar, add the egg and combine to form a dough. Wrap in clear film (plastic wrap) and chill for 1 hour.

2 Preheat the oven to 180°C/350°F/Gas 4. On a lightly floured surface, roll out the pastry thinly and use to line a 20cm/8in flan tin (pan).

3 Put a circle of baking parchment in the pastry case (pie shell) and fill with baking beans. Bake in the oven for 10–15 minutes until the pastry has set. Remove the paper and beans and return to the oven for 5 minutes until the base is dry.

4 Fill the tart with the berries and sugar. Return to the oven and bake for a further 5–10 minutes until the pastry is golden brown. Serve warm, with cream.

Nutritional information per portion: Energy 618kcal/2601kJ; Protein 8g; Carbohydrate 98.1g, of which sugars 43.3g; Fat 24.2g, of which saturates 14.9g; Cholesterol 60mg; Calcium 141mg; Fibre 3.8g; Sodium 177mg.

Raspberry and almond tart

Juicy ripe raspberries and almonds go very well together in this dish. This is a rich tart, ideal for serving at the end of a special lunch or at a dinner party.

SERVES 4

200g/7oz ready-made sweet shortcrust pastry
2 large (US extra large) eggs
75ml/2½ fl oz/⅓ cup double (heavy) cream
50g/2oz/¼ cup caster (superfine) sugar
50g/2oz/½ cup ground almonds
20g/¾oz/4 tsp butter
350g/12oz/2 cups raspberries

1 Line a 20cm/8in flan tin (pan) with the pastry. Prick the base all over and leave to rest for at least 30 minutes. Preheat the oven to 200°C/400°F/Gas 6.

2 Put the eggs, cream, sugar and ground almonds in a bowl and whisk together briskly. Melt the butter and pour into the mixture, stirring to combine thoroughly.

3 Sprinkle the raspberries evenly over the pastry case. The ones at the top will appear through the surface, so keep them evenly spaced. You can also create a pattern with them.

4 Pour the egg and almond mixture over the top. Once again ensure that it is spread evenly throughout the tart. Bake in the preheated oven for 25 minutes. Serve warm or cold.

Nutritional information per portion: Energy 548kcal/2284kJ; Protein 10.9g; Carbohydrate 41.7g, of which sugars 18.4g; Fat 38.8g, of which saturates 14.8g; Cholesterol 158mg; Calcium 128mg; Fibre 4.1g; Sodium 282mg.

Almond tart

This dessert comes from Portugal, where many variations of the recipe exist. It uses partly unpeeled almonds for additional flavour. Serve with a raspberry sorbet.

SERVES 12

melted butter, for brushing
40g/1½ oz/¾ cup breadcrumbs, plus
    extra for sprinkling
200g/7oz/1¾ cups shelled almonds
500g/1¼ lb/generous 2¾ cups sugar
50g/2oz/¼ cup butter
4 eggs
6 egg yolks
icing (confectioners') sugar, to decorate
raspberry sorbet, to serve

1 Preheat the oven to 160°C/325°F/ Gas 3. Brush a round cake tin (pan), 25cm/10in in diameter and 5cm/2in deep, with melted butter, then line with baking parchment. Brush with butter again. Sprinkle with breadcrumbs, shaking out the excess.

2 Place half the almonds in a heatproof bowl and pour in boiling water to cover. Leave to stand for a few minutes, then drain and rub off the skins. In a food processor, process all the almonds to crumbs.

3 Put the sugar in a pan, add 250ml/ 8fl oz/1 cup water and bring to the boil, stirring until the sugar has dissolved, then boil, without stirring, until a thick syrup forms. Remove from the heat. Stir in the butter.

4 Mix together the eggs, egg yolks, almonds and breadcrumbs in a bowl, then stir into the syrup. Spoon into the prepared tin and bake for 1 hour, until just firm but still moist. Turn out on to a rack to cool. Sprinkle with icing sugar and serve with the sorbet.

Nutritional information per portion: Energy 364kcal/1529kJ; Protein 7.7g; Carbohydrate 47.3g, of which sugars 44.4g; Fat 17.4g, of which saturates 4.2g; Cholesterol 173mg; Calcium 88mg; Fibre 1.3g; Sodium 83mg.

American pumpkin pie

This spicy sweet pie is traditionally served at Thanksgiving, or at Halloween as a way to use the pulp from the hollowed-out pumpkin lanterns.

SERVES 8

900g/2lb piece of pumpkin
2 large (US extra large) eggs
75g/3oz/scant ½ cup soft light
   brown sugar
60ml/4 tbsp golden (light corn) syrup
250ml/8fl oz/1 cup double (heavy) cream
15ml/1 tbsp mixed (pumpkin pie) spice
2.5ml/½ tsp salt
icing (confectioners') sugar, for dusting

FOR THE PASTRY

200g/7oz/1¾ cups plain
   (all-purpose) flour
2.5ml/½ tsp salt
90g/3½ oz/scant ½ cup butter, diced
1 egg yolk
15ml/1 tbsp chilled water

1 To make the pastry, sift the flour and salt into a bowl. Rub in the butter, then mix in the egg yolk and enough chilled water to make a soft dough. Roll into a ball, wrap it in clear film (plastic wrap) and chill for 30 minutes.

2 Peel and seed the pumpkin. Cut the flesh into cubes. Place in a pan and cover with water. Bring to the boil and simmer for 15–20 minutes until tender. Mash well until smooth, then spoon into a sieve (strainer) and set over a bowl to drain. Preheat the oven to 200°C/400°F/Gas 6.

3 Roll out the pastry. Line a 23cm/ 9in loose-based flan tin (pan). Prick the base all over. Line with foil and baking beans. Chill for 15 minutes. Bake for 10 minutes, remove the foil and beans, then bake for a further 5 minutes.

4 Lower the oven temperature to 190°C/375°F/Gas 5. Put the pumpkin into a bowl and beat in the eggs, sugar, syrup, cream, mixed spice and salt to make a smooth filling. Pour into the pastry case. Bake for 40 minutes until set. Dust generously with icing sugar. Serve at room temperature.

Nutritional information per portion: Energy 416kcal/1736kJ; Protein 5.3g; Carbohydrate 38.2g, of which sugars 18.6g; Fat 28g, of which saturates 16.9g; Cholesterol 114mg; Calcium 98mg; Fibre 1.9g; Sodium 360mg.

Lemon tart

This classic French tart is one of the most delicious desserts there is. A rich lemon curd is contained in a crisp pastry case. Crème fraîche is an optional – but nice – extra.

SERVES 6

6 eggs, beaten
350g/12oz/1½ cups caster
    (superfine) sugar
115g/4oz/½ cup butter
grated rind and juice of 4 lemons
icing (confectioners') sugar, for dusting

FOR THE PASTRY
225g/8oz/2 cups plain (all-purpose) flour
115g/4oz/½ cup butter, diced
30ml/2 tbsp icing (confectioners') sugar
1 egg
5ml/1 tsp vanilla extract
15ml/1 tbsp chilled water

1 Preheat the oven to 200°C/400°F/Gas 6. To make the pastry, sift the flour into a mixing bowl and rub in the butter. Stir in the icing sugar. Add the egg, vanilla extract and most of the chilled water, then work to a soft dough. Add a few more drops of water if necessary. Knead quickly and lightly until smooth.

2 Roll out the pastry on a floured surface and use to line a 23cm/9in flan tin (pan). Prick the base all over with a fork. Line with baking parchment and fill with baking beans. Bake the pastry case for 10 minutes. Remove the paper and beans and set the pastry case aside while you make the filling.

3 Put the eggs, sugar and butter into a pan, and stir over a low heat until all the sugar has dissolved. Add the lemon rind and juice, and continue cooking, stirring constantly, until it has thickened slightly. Pour the mixture into the pastry case.

4 Bake for 20 minutes, until the filling is just set. Transfer the tart to a wire rack to cool. Dust the surface generously with icing sugar just before serving.

Nutritional information per portion: Energy 268kcal/1121kJ; Protein 5.6g; Carbohydrate 27g, of which sugars 10.9g; Fat 16.1g, of which saturates 5.8g; Cholesterol 148mg; Calcium 57mg; Fibre 0.7g; Sodium 173mg.

Lemon meringue pie

This popular dessert is a 20th-century development of older English cheesecakes – open tarts with a filling of fruit curds. The pie is best served at room temperature, with or without cream.

SERVES 6

FOR THE PASTRY
115g/4oz/1 cup plain (all-purpose) flour
a pinch of salt
25g/1oz/2 tbsp lard or white cooking fat, diced
25g/1oz/2 tbsp butter, diced

FOR THE FILLING
50g/2oz/¼ cup cornflour (cornstarch)
175g/6oz/¾ cup caster (superfine) sugar
finely grated rind and juice of 2 lemons
2 egg yolks
15g/½oz/1 tbsp butter, diced

FOR THE MERINGUE TOPPING
2 egg whites
75g/3oz/½ cup caster (superfine) sugar

1 To make the pastry, sift the flour and salt into a bowl and add the lard or fat and butter. With the fingertips, lightly rub the fats into the flour until the mixture resembles fine crumbs.

2 Stir in about 20ml/2 tbsp cold water until the mixture can be gathered together into a smooth ball of dough. (Alternatively make the pastry using a food processor.) Wrap in clear film (plastic wrap) and chill for at least 30 minutes. Meanwhile, preheat the oven to 200°C/400°F/Gas 6.

3 Roll out the pastry on a lightly floured surface and use to line a 20cm/8in flan tin (pan). Prick the base with a fork, line with baking parchment or foil and add a layer of baking beans.

4 Put the pastry case (pie shell) into the hot oven and cook for 15 minutes. Remove the beans and parchment or foil, return the pastry to the oven and cook for a further 5 minutes until crisp and golden brown. Reduce the oven temperature to 150°C/300°F/Gas 2.

5 To make the lemon filling, put the cornflour into a pan and add the sugar, lemon rind and 300ml/½ pint/1¼ cups water. Heat the mixture, stirring constantly, until it comes to the boil and thickens. Reduce the heat and simmer very gently for 1 minute. Remove the pan from the heat and stir in the lemon juice.

6 Add the the egg yolks to the lemon mixture, one at a time and beating after each addition, and then stir in the butter. Pour the mixture into the baked pastry case and level the surface.

7 To make the meringue topping, whisk the egg whites until stiff peaks form, then whisk in half the sugar. Fold in the rest of the sugar using a metal spoon.

8 Spread the meringue over the lemon filling, covering it completely. Cook for about 20 minutes until lightly browned.

Nutritional information per portion: Energy 357kcal/1497kJ; Protein 6.8g; Carbohydrate 42.8g, of which sugars 25.1g; Fat 18.9g, of which saturates 9g; Cholesterol 129mg; Calcium 108mg; Fibre 0.7g; Sodium 137mg.

Treacle tart

Traditional shortcrust pastry is perfect for this old-fashioned favourite, with its sticky lemon and golden syrup filling and twisted lattice topping.

SERVES 4–6

260g/9½ oz/generous ¾ cup golden
 (light corn) syrup
75g/3oz/1½ cups fresh
 white breadcrumbs
grated rind of 1 lemon
30ml/2 tbsp lemon juice
custard, to serve

FOR THE PASTRY

150g/5oz/1¼ cups plain
 (all-purpose) flour
2.5ml/½ tsp salt
130g/4½ oz/9 tbsp chilled
 butter, diced
45–60ml/3–4 tbsp chilled water

1 To make the pastry, combine the flour and salt in a bowl. Rub in the butter. With a fork, stir in just enough water to bind the dough. Gather into a smooth ball and knead lightly until smooth. Wrap in clear film (plastic wrap). Chill for at least 20 minutes.

2 On a lightly floured surface, roll out the pastry to 3mm/⅛in thick. Transfer to a 20cm/8in fluted flan tin (pan) and trim off the overhang. Chill the pastry case for 20 minutes. Reserve the trimmings. Put a baking sheet in the oven and preheat to 200°C/400°F/Gas 6. Warm the syrup in a pan until it melts.

3 Remove the syrup from the heat. Stir in the breadcrumbs and lemon rind. Leave to stand for 10 minutes, then add more breadcrumbs if too moist and thin. Stir in the lemon juice, and spread evenly in the pastry case.

4 Roll out the pastry trimmings and cut into 10–12 thin strips. Twist the strips into spirals. Lay half of them on the filling. Arrange the remaining strips at right angles to form a lattice. Press the ends on to the rim. Bake the tart on the hot baking sheet for 10 minutes. Lower the oven to 190°C/375°F/Gas 5. Bake for 15 minutes, until golden. Serve warm with custard.

Nutritional information per portion: Energy 418Kcal/1747kJ; Protein 4.4g; Carbohydrate 61g, of which sugars 12.3g; Fat 18.3g, of which saturates 11.3g; Cholesterol 46mg; Calcium 26mg; Fibre 1.2g; Sodium 217mg.

Boston banoffee pie

Simply press this wonderfully biscuity pastry into the tin, rather than rolling it out. Add the fudge-toffee filling and sliced banana topping and it'll prove irresistible.

SERVES 6

115g/4oz/½ cup butter, diced

200g/7oz can skimmed, sweetened condensed milk

115g/4oz/½ cup soft light brown sugar

30ml/2 tbsp golden (light corn) syrup

2 small bananas, sliced

a little lemon juice

whipped cream, to decorate

5ml/1 tsp grated plain (semisweet) chocolate, to decorate

FOR THE PASTRY

150g/5oz/1¼ cups plain (all-purpose) flour

115g/4oz/½ cup butter, diced

50g/2oz/¼ cup caster (superfine) sugar

1 Preheat the oven to 160°C/325°F/ Gas 3. To make the pastry, in a food processor, process the flour and diced butter until crumbed. Stir in the caster sugar and mix to form a soft, pliable dough. Press the dough into a 20cm/8in loose-based flan tin (pan) and bake for 30 minutes.

2 To make the filling, place the butter in a pan with the condensed milk, brown sugar and syrup. Heat gently, stirring, until the butter has melted and the sugar has dissolved.

3 Bring to a gentle boil and cook for 7–10 minutes, stirring constantly, until the mixture thickens and turns a light caramel colour. Pour the hot caramel filling into the pastry case and leave until completely cold.

4 Sprinkle the banana slices with lemon juice and arrange in overlapping circles on top of the filling, leaving a gap in the centre. Pipe a generous swirl of whipped cream in the centre and sprinkle with grated chocolate.

Nutritional information per portion: Energy 608kcal/2547kJ; Protein 6.4g; Carbohydrate 78.5g, of which sugars 58.9g; Fat 32g, of which saturates 20.1g; Cholesterol 82mg; Calcium 169mg; Fibre 1.1g; Sodium 299mg.

Mississippi mud pie

Mud, mud, glorious mud – isn't that what the song says? Well, you can't get much more glorious than this – its status as a popular classic is definitely well earned.

SERVES 6–8

250g/9oz/2¼ cups plain (all-purpose) flour
150g/5oz/⅔ cup unsalted butter
2 egg yolks
15–30ml/1–2 tbsp chilled water

FOR THE FILLING
3 eggs, separated
20ml/4 tsp cornflour (cornstarch)
75g/3oz/⅓ cup caster (superfine) sugar
400ml/14fl oz/1¾ cups full cream (whole) milk

150g/5oz plain (semisweet) chocolate,
   broken into squares
5ml/1 tsp vanilla extract
1 sachet powdered gelatine
45ml/3 tbsp water
30ml/2 tsp dark rum

FOR THE TOPPING
175g/6fl oz/¾ cup double (heavy) cream, whipped
chocolate curls, to decorate

1 Sift the flour into a bowl and rub in the butter until the mixture resembles coarse breadcrumbs. Stir in the egg yolks with just enough chilled water to bind the mixture to a soft dough. Roll out on a lightly floured surface and line a deep 23cm/9in flan tin (pan). Chill for about 30 minutes.

2 Preheat the oven to 190°C/375°F/Gas 5. Prick the pastry with a fork, cover with baking parchment weighed down with baking beans and bake blind for 10 minutes. Remove the baking beans and paper, return to the oven and bake for a further 10 minutes, until the pastry is crisp and golden. Cool in the tin.

3 For the filling, mix the egg yolks, cornflour and 30ml/2 tbsp of the sugar in a bowl. Heat the milk in a pan until almost boiling, then beat into the egg mixture. Return to a clean pan and stir over a low heat until the custard is smooth and thick. Pour half the custard into a bowl. Melt the chocolate in a heatproof bowl over simmering water, then stir into the custard in the bowl, with the vanilla extract. Spread in the pastry case, cover closely to prevent the formation of a skin, cool, then chill until set.

4 Sprinkle the gelatine over the water in a heatproof bowl, leave until spongy, then place over simmering water until all the gelatine has dissolved. Stir into the remaining custard, with the rum.

5 Whisk the egg whites until stiff peaks form, whisk in the remaining sugar, then fold quickly into the custard before it sets. Spoon over the chocolate custard. Chill until set, then remove the pie from the tin and place on a serving plate. Spread whipped cream over the top and sprinkle with chocolate curls.

Nutritional information per portion: Energy 571kcal/2385kJ; Protein 9.4g; Carbohydrate 53.5g, of which sugars 22.7g; Fat 36.2g, of which saturates 21.2g; Cholesterol 196mg; Calcium 160mg; Fibre 1.3g; Sodium 180mg.

Key lime pie

This pie is a classic American favourite. As the name suggests, it originated in the Florida Keys, but it is now a hugely popular pie all over the world.

SERVES 10

4 eggs, separated
400g/14oz can skimmed, sweetened
    condensed milk
grated rind and juice of 3 limes
a few drops of green food colouring
30ml/2 tbsp caster (superfine) sugar
300ml/½ pint/1¼ cups double
    (heavy) cream
2–3 limes, thinly sliced
thinly pared lime rind and fresh mint
    sprigs, to decorate

FOR THE PASTRY

225g/8oz/2 cups plain (all-purpose) flour
115g/4oz/½ cup chilled butter, diced
30ml/2 tbsp caster (superfine) sugar
a pinch of salt
2 egg yolks
30ml/2 tbsp chilled water

1 To make the pastry, sift the flour into a bowl and rub in the butter. Add the sugar, salt, egg yolks and enough water to bind. Knead to a soft dough, then roll out thinly and use to line a deep 21cm/8½in fluted flan tin (pan). Allow the excess to overhang the edge. Prick the base all over, wrap in clear film (plastic wrap) and chill for 30 minutes. Preheat the oven to 200°C/400°F/Gas 6.

2 Trim off the excess pastry from around the edge of the pastry case, then line with baking parchment and fill with baking beans. Bake for 10 minutes, remove the beans and parchment and bake for 10 minutes more until lightly brown.

3 Beat the egg yolks until light and creamy, then beat in the condensed milk, lime rind and juice. Add the food colouring, and beat until the mixture is thick. Whisk the egg whites in a grease-free bowl until stiff peaks form. Whisk in the sugar, then fold into the lime mixture. Reduce the oven to 160°C/325°F/Gas 3.

4 Pour the filling into the case. Bake for 20 minutes. Cool, then chill. Whip the cream and spoon around the edge. Add lime twists and rind, and mint sprigs.

Nutritional information per portion: Energy 510kcal/2126kJ; Protein 9.2g; Carbohydrate 46.6g, of which sugars 29.4g; Fat 33.2g, of which saturates 19.5g; Cholesterol 196mg; Calcium 182mg; Fibre 0.7g; Sodium 163mg.

Cappuccino torte

The famous and much-loved beverage of freshly brewed coffee, whipped cream, chocolate and cinnamon is transformed into a sensational dessert.

SERVES 6–8

75g/3oz/6 tbsp butter, melted

275g/10oz shortbread biscuits
(cookies), crushed

1.5ml/¼ tsp ground cinnamon

25ml/1½ tbsp powdered gelatine

45ml/3 tbsp cold water

2 eggs, separated

115g/4oz/½ cup soft light brown sugar

115g/4oz plain (semisweet)
chocolate, chopped

175ml/6fl oz/¾ cup hot
brewed espresso

400ml/14fl oz/1⅔ cups whipping cream

grated chocolate and ground cinnamon,
to decorate

1 Mix the butter with the biscuits and cinnamon. Spoon into the base of a 20cm/8in loose-based flan tin (pan) and press down well. Chill.

2 Sprinkle the gelatine over the cold water. Leave to soften for 5 minutes, then place the bowl over a pan of hot water and stir to dissolve.

3 Whisk the egg yolks and sugar until thick. Put the chocolate in a bowl with the coffee and stir until melted. Add to the egg mixture, then cook gently in a pan, stirring constantly, for 1–2 minutes until thickened. Stir in the gelatine. Leave until just beginning to set, stirring occasionally.

4 Whip 150ml/¼ pint/⅔ cup of the cream until soft peaks form. Whisk the egg whites until stiff. Fold the cream into the coffee mixture, followed by the egg whites. Pour the mixture over the biscuit base and chill for 2 hours.

5 To serve, remove from the tin and transfer to a serving plate. Whip the rest of the cream and dollop it on top. Decorate with grated chocolate and cinnamon.

Nutritional information per portion: Energy 584kcal/2429kJ; Protein 5.5g; Carbohydrate 47.3g, of which sugars 30.8g; Fat 42.7g, of which saturates 26.6g; Cholesterol 146mg; Calcium 81mg; Fibre 1g; Sodium 181mg.

Classic American creamy cheesecake

There are a million cheesecake recipes, including ones that are topped with fruit or scented with lemon, but this classic version makes the perfect dessert for a family meal.

SERVES 6–8

130g/4¹/2oz/generous ¹/2 cup butter, melted, plus extra for greasing
350g/12oz digestive biscuits (graham crackers), finely crushed
350–400g/12–14oz/1³/4–2 cups caster (superfine) sugar
350g/12oz/1¹/2 cups full-fat soft white (farmer's) cheese
3 eggs, lightly beaten
15ml/1 tbsp vanilla extract
350g/12oz/1¹/2 cups sour cream
strawberries, blueberries, raspberries and icing (confectioners') sugar, to serve

1 Butter a deep 23cm/9in springform tin (pan). Put the biscuit crumbs and 60ml/4 tbsp of the sugar in a bowl and mix together, then add the melted butter and mix well. Press the mixture into the tin to cover the base and sides. Chill for 30 minutes.

2 Preheat the oven to 190°C/375°F/ Gas 5. Using an electric mixer, food processor or wooden spoon, beat the cheese until soft. Beat in the eggs, then 250g/9oz/1¹/2 cups of the sugar and 10ml/2 tsp of the vanilla extract.

3 Pour the mixture over the crumb base and bake for 45 minutes, or until a cocktail stick (toothpick), inserted in the centre, comes out clean. Leave to cool slightly for about 10 minutes. (Do not turn the oven off.)

4 Combine the sour cream and remaining sugar, to taste. Stir in the remaining vanilla extract. Spread evenly on the cheesecake. Return to the oven and bake for 5 minutes. Cool, then chill. Serve with the fresh berries, and dusted with icing sugar.

Nutritional information per portion: Energy 634kcal/2628kJ; Protein 7.8g; Carbohydrate 31.8g, of which sugars 7.7g; Fat 53.8g, of which saturates 31.5g; Cholesterol 192mg; Calcium 137mg; Fibre 1g; Sodium 536mg.

Baked Polish cheesecake

Cheesecake is popular in Poland, and there are many versions of it there. This particular recipe is very light as it is not made on a biscuit base.

SERVES 6–8

500g/1¼ lb/2¼ cups curd
    (farmer's) cheese
100g/3¾oz/scant ½ cup butter, softened
2.5ml/½ tsp vanilla extract
6 eggs, separated
150g/5oz/¾ cup caster (superfine) sugar
10ml/2 tsp grated lemon rind
15ml/1 tbsp cornflour (cornstarch)
15ml/1 tbsp semolina
50g/5oz/⅓ cup raisins or sultanas
    (golden raisins) (optional)
icing (confectioners') sugar, to dust

1 Preheat the oven to 200°C/400°F/ Gas 6. Grease and line a 20cm/8in round cake tin (pan). Cream together the curd cheese, butter and vanilla in a large bowl until combined.

2 In a separate large bowl, whisk the egg whites with 15ml/1 tbsp sugar, until stiff peaks form.

3 In a third bowl, whisk the egg yolks with the remaining sugar until the mixture is thick and creamy.

4 Add the egg yolk and sugar mixture to the curd cheese and butter mixture with the lemon rind and stir to combine. Gently fold in the egg whites, then the cornflour, semolina and raisins or sultanas, if using.

5 Transfer the mixture to the prepared tin and bake for 1 hour, or until set and golden brown.

6 Leave to cool in the tin, then dust with icing sugar and serve in slices.

Nutritional information per portion: Energy 347kcal/1448kJ; Protein 10.8g; Carbohydrate 24.8g, of which sugars 21.6g; Fat 23.6g, of which saturates 13.4g; Cholesterol 196mg; Calcium 34mg; Fibre 0g; Sodium 131mg.

Cheesecake with sour cherries

This is a Belgian cheesecake with a rich, creamy texture. The base is made using Belgium's favourite cookie, speculaas, while the topping is spiked with cherry-flavoured beer.

SERVES 6

500g/1¼ lb jar stoned (pitted) Morello
    cherries in syrup
60m/4 tbsp water
30ml/2 tbsp powdered gelatine
150ml/¼ pint/⅔ cup cherry-flavoured
    beer, such as St. Louis, Belle-Vue
    or Lindemans
500g/1¼ lb/2¼ cups Quark, soft white
    (farmer's) cheese or fromage frais
150ml/¼ pint/⅔ cup crème fraîche or
    sour cream

200ml/7fl oz/scant 1 cup double (heavy) cream
115g/4oz/generous ½ cup caster
    (superfine) sugar
90ml/6 tbsp flaked (sliced) almonds,
    to decorate (optional)

FOR THE CRUST

200g/7oz speculaas cookies (spice cookies)
    or other cookies suitable for crumbing
100g/3½ oz/scant ½ cup unsalted butter
30ml/2 tbsp cherry jam (optional)

1 Make the crust. Crumb the cookies in a food processor or put them between sheets of baking parchment and crush with a rolling pin. Put into a bowl.

2 Melt the butter in a pan and stir it into the crumbs with the jam, if using. Mix well. Using clean hands, shape into a ball.

3 Place in a 23cm/9in springform cake tin (pan) and press out to form an even base. Cover with clear film (plastic wrap) and place in the refrigerator.

4 Drain the cherries in a colander, reserving the syrup in a measuring jug (cup). Chop 115g/4oz/ ⅔ cup of the cherries and set them aside. Leave the remaining cherries in the colander.

5 Put the water in a cup and sprinkle the gelatine on the surface. Leave until spongy.

6 Pour 150ml/¼ pint/⅔ cup of the syrup from the cherries into a pan. Bring to the boil, then cool for 30 seconds. Whisk in the gelatine until dissolved. Stir in the beer and strain the mixture into a jug (pitcher).

7 In a large bowl, beat the Quark, soft cheese or fromage frais with the crème fraîche or sour cream, and gradually add the gelatine mixture. Fold in the reserved chopped cherries.

8 Whip the cream with the sugar in a bowl, until stiff peaks form. Carefully fold it into the cheese mixture.

9 Spoon the filling over the crumb base in the tin and smooth the top with a wetted spoon or spatula. Cover with clear film. Chill in the refrigerator for at least 4 hours or overnight.

10 Remove the cheesecake from the tin and transfer it to a serving platter. Sprinkle the flaked almonds over the surface of the cheesecake and press some on to the sides. Serve in slices, with the drained cherries.

Nutritional information per portion: Energy 574kcal/2394kJ; Protein 6.5g; Carbohydrate 50.1g, of which sugars 39g; Fat 39.5g, of which saturates 24.9g; Cholesterol 87mg; Calcium 145mg; Fibre 0.7g; Sodium 198mg.

Raspberry, mascarpone and white chocolate cheesecake

Raspberries and white chocolate are an irresistible combination, especially when teamed with rich mascarpone on a crunchy ginger and pecan nut base.

SERVES 8

50g/2oz/4 tbsp unsalted butter
225g/8oz ginger nut biscuits
   (gingersnaps), crushed
50g/2oz/1/2 cup chopped pecan nuts

250g/9oz white chocolate, broken
   into squares
225g/8oz/11/2 cups fresh or
   frozen raspberries

FOR THE FILLING
275g/10oz/11/4 cups mascarpone
175g/6oz/3/4 cup fromage frais or ricotta
2 eggs, beaten
45ml/3 tbsp caster (superfine) sugar

FOR THE TOPPING
115g/4oz/1/2 cup mascarpone
75g/3oz/1/3 cup fromage frais or ricotta
white chocolate curls and raspberries,
   to decorate

1 Preheat the oven to 150°C/300°F/Gas 2. Melt the butter in a pan, then stir in the crushed biscuits and nuts. Press into the base of a 23cm/9in springform cake tin (pan).

2 Make the filling. Beat the mascarpone and fromage frais or ricotta in a bowl, then beat in the eggs and caster sugar until evenly mixed.

3 Melt the white chocolate gently in a heatproof bowl over simmering water, then stir into the cheese mixture with the fresh or frozen raspberries.

4 Turn into the prepared tin and spread evenly, then bake for about 1 hour or until just set. Switch off the oven, but do not remove the cheesecake. Leave it until cold and completely set.

5 Remove the sides of the tin and carefully lift the cheesecake on to a serving plate. Make the topping by mixing the mascarpone and fromage frais or ricotta in a bowl, then spread the mixture over the cheesecake. Decorate with chocolate curls and raspberries.

Nutritional information per portion: Energy 551kcal/2305kJ; Protein 12.8g; Carbohydrate 53.9g, of which sugars 41.4g; Fat 33.1g, of which saturates 17g; Cholesterol 88mg; Calcium 170mg; Fibre 1.4g; Sodium 195mg.

Cakes, gateaux and pastries

Often reserved for afternoon tea, cakes and gateaux can also feature on the dessert menu, especially when they are oozing with indulgent creamy fillings, as in the case of Cinnamon Apple Gateau and Layer Cake with Cream and Raspberries. Gooey chocolate cakes also feature in this chapter, as do elegant roulades, pretty choux pastries, for example Chocolate Éclairs and Chocolate Profiteroles, and crispy filo desserts, including Baklava.

Plum cake

This cardamom-accented cake has an intriguing pale bluish-green hue from the plum skins, and lovely almond undertones to its fruity flavour.

SERVES 10

450g/1lb stoned (pitted) fresh plums,
    coarsely chopped, plus 9 extra plums,
    stoned and halved, to decorate
300ml/1/2 pint/11/4 cups water
115g/4oz/1/2 cup unsalted butter, softened
200g/7oz/1 cup caster (superfine) sugar
3 eggs
90g/31/2 oz/3/4 cup toasted,
    finely chopped almonds

5ml/1 tsp bicarbonate of soda (baking soda)
7.5ml/11/2 tsp baking powder
5ml/1 tsp ground cardamom
1.5ml/1/4 tsp salt
250g/9oz/21/4 cups plain (all-purpose) flour
15ml/1 tbsp pearl sugar, to decorate
250ml/8fl oz/1 cup double (heavy) cream
10ml/2 tsp vanilla sugar
10ml/2 tsp icing (confectioners') sugar

1 Place the chopped plums in a pan and add the water. Bring to the boil over a medium heat and cook for 10–15 minutes, until soft. Set aside to cool. You will need 350ml/12fl oz/11/2 cups stewed plums for the cake.

2 Preheat the oven to 180°C/350°F/Gas 4. Grease and flour a 24cm/91/2in springform cake tin (pan).

3 Cream the butter with the sugar in a mixing bowl until light and fluffy. Beat in the eggs, one at a time. Stir in the stewed plums and the almonds. Add the bicarbonate of soda, baking powder, cardamom and salt and stir until blended. Gradually stir in the flour, a few spoons at a time, and mix until incorporated.

4 Pour the mixture into the prepared tin. Place 15 plum halves around the circumference of the cake and the remaining three halves in the centre, cut sides down. Sprinkle the pearl sugar over the cake. Bake for 1 hour, or until the top springs back when lightly touched. Cool in the tin for 15 minutes before unfastening the ring.

5 Beat the double cream until soft peaks form. Stir in the vanilla sugar and the icing sugar, and beat until thick. Serve the cake, still slightly warm, or at room temperature, in slices with a dollop of whipped cream.

Nutritional information per portion: Energy 311kcal/1308kJ; Protein 6.4g; Carbohydrate 44.5g, of which sugars 15.9g; Fat 13.2g, of which saturates 7.4g; Cholesterol 89mg; Calcium 86mg; Fibre 2.4g; Sodium 102mg.

Moist orange and almond cake

The key to this recipe is to cook the orange slowly first, so it is fully tender before being blended. Don't use a microwave to speed things up – this makes orange skin tough.

SERVES 8

1 large orange
3 eggs
225g/8oz/1 cup caster (superfine) sugar
5ml/1 tsp baking powder
225g/8oz/2 cups ground almonds
25g/1oz/¼ cup plain (all-purpose) flour
icing (confectioners') sugar, for dusting
whipped cream and orange slices
**   (optional), to serve**

COOK'S TIP
For a treat, serve this with spiced poached kumquats.

1 Wash the orange and pierce it with a skewer. Put it in a deep pan and pour over water to cover completely. Bring to the boil then lower the heat, cover and simmer for 1 hour or until the skin is very soft. Drain, then cool.

2 Preheat the oven to 180°C/350°F/Gas 4. Grease a 20cm/8in round cake tin (pan) and line it with baking parchment. Cut the cooled orange in half and discard the pips (seeds). Place the orange, skin and all, in a blender or food processor and purée until smooth and pulpy.

3 In a bowl, whisk the eggs and sugar until thick. Fold in the baking powder, almonds and flour. Fold in the purée.

4 Pour into the prepared tin, level the surface and bake for 1 hour or until a skewer inserted into the middle comes out clean. Cool the cake in the tin for 10 minutes, then turn out on to a wire rack, peel off the lining paper and cool completely. Dust the top liberally with icing sugar and tuck orange slices under the cake just before serving, if you like, with whipped cream.

Nutritional information per portion: Energy 187kcal/783kJ; Protein 5.1g; Carbohydrate 20g, of which sugars 18.2g; Fat 10.2g, of which saturates 1.1g; Cholesterol 41mg; Calcium 60mg; Fibre 1.4g; Sodium 19mg.

Lemon and lime syrup cake

This recipe is perfect for busy cooks as it can be mixed in moments. The simple, tangy lime topping soaks into the cake, making it fabulously moist.

SERVES 8

225g/8oz/2 cups self-raising
  (self-rising) flour
5ml/1 tsp baking powder
225g/8oz/1 cup caster (superfine) sugar
225g/8oz/1 cup butter, softened
4 eggs, beaten
grated rind of 2 lemons
30ml/2 tbsp lemon juice

FOR THE TOPPING

finely pared rind of 1 lime
juice of 2 limes
150g/5oz/²⁄₃ cup caster (superfine) sugar

VARIATION

Use the rind and juice of 1 lemon for the topping, if you prefer.

1 Make the cake. Preheat the oven to 160°C/325°F/Gas 3. Grease and line a 20cm/8in round cake tin (pan). Sift the flour and baking powder into a large bowl. Add the caster sugar, butter and eggs and beat together well until the mixture is smooth, creamy and fluffy.

2 Beat in the lemon rind and juice. Spoon the mixture into the prepared tin, then smooth the surface and make a shallow indentation in the top with the back of a spoon.

3 Bake for 1¹⁄₄–1¹⁄₂ hours or until the cake is golden on top and spongy when lightly pressed, and a skewer inserted in the centre comes out clean.

4 Meanwhile, mix the topping ingredients together. As soon as the cake is cooked, remove it from the oven and pour the topping over the surface. Allow the cake to cool in the tin.

Nutritional information per portion: Energy 527kcal/2209kJ; Protein 6.2g; Carbohydrate 71g, of which sugars 49.6g; Fat 26.3g, of which saturates 15.5g; Cholesterol 155mg; Calcium 84mg; Fibre 0.9g; Sodium 209mg.

Cinnamon apple gateau

Make this unusual cake for an autumn celebration. A light sponge is split and filled with a honey and cream cheese layer, as well as cinnamon, apples and sultanas, then topped with glazed apples.

SERVES 8–10

butter, for greasing
3 eggs
115g/4oz/generous ½ cup caster
   (superfine) sugar
75g/3oz/²⁄₃ cup plain (all-purpose) flour
5ml/1 tsp ground cinnamon

FOR THE FILLING AND TOPPING

4 large eating apples
60ml/4 tbsp clear honey
75g/3oz/generous ½ cup sultanas (golden raisins)
2.5ml/½ tsp ground cinnamon
350g/12oz/1½ cups soft cheese
60ml/4 tbsp fromage frais or crème fraîche
10ml/2 tsp lemon juice
45ml/3 tbsp apricot glaze (apricot jam and a
   little water, boiled and strained)
mint sprigs, to decorate

1 Preheat the oven to 190°C/375°F/Gas 5. Grease and line a 23cm/9in round cake tin (pan) with baking parchment.

2 Put the eggs and sugar in a bowl and beat with an electric whisk until thick and mousse-like and the beaters leave a trail on the surface.

3 Sift the flour and cinnamon over the egg mixture and carefully fold in with a large metal spoon.

4 Pour into the prepared tin and bake for 25–30 minutes, or until the cake springs back when lightly pressed in the centre.

5 Slide a knife between the cake and the tin to loosen the edge, then turn the cake out on to a wire rack to cool.

6 To make the filling, peel, core and slice three of the apples and put them in a pan. Add 30ml/ 2 tbsp of the honey and 15ml/1 tbsp water. Cover and cook over a low heat for 10 minutes, or until the apples have softened. Add the sultanas and cinnamon, stir, replace the lid and leave to cool.

7 Put the soft cheese in a bowl with the remaining honey, the fromage frais or crème fraîche and half the lemon juice. Beat until smooth.

8 Cut the cake into two equal rounds. Put half on a plate and drizzle over any liquid from the apples.

9 Spread with two-thirds of the cheese mixture, then top with the apple filling. Fit the top of the cake in place.

10 Swirl the remaining cheese mixture over the top of the sponge. Core and slice the remaining apple, sprinkle with lemon juice and use to decorate the edge of the cake. Brush the apple with apricot glaze and place the mint sprigs on top.

Nutritional information per portion: Energy 239kcal/1010kJ; Protein 10.8g; Carbohydrate 39.9g, of which sugars 32.8g; Fat 5.8g, of which saturates 2.9g; Cholesterol 82mg; Calcium 97mg; Fibre 1.1g; Sodium 225mg.

Apple cake

This moist cake has a lovely crunchy top and can either be served cold, as a cake, or warm with chilled cream or custard as a scrumptious dessert.

SERVES 10

225g/8oz/2 cups self-raising
   (self-rising) flour
a large pinch of salt
a pinch of ground cloves
115g/4oz/½ cup butter,
   at room temperature
4 cooking apples
115g/4oz/generous ½ cup caster
   (superfine) sugar
2 eggs, beaten
a little milk to mix
granulated (white) sugar, for sprinkling

1 Preheat the oven to 190°C/375°F/Gas 5 and grease a 20cm/8in cake tin (pan) with butter.

2 Sift the flour, salt and ground cloves into a bowl. Rub in the butter until the mixture is like fine breadcrumbs. Peel and core the apples. Slice them thinly and add to the rubbed-in mixture with the sugar.

3 Mix in the eggs and enough milk to make a fairly stiff dough, then turn the mixture into the prepared tin and sprinkle with granulated sugar.

4 Bake in the preheated oven for 30–40 minutes, or until springy to the touch and a skewer, inserted into the centre, comes out clean. Cool on a wire rack.

Nutritional information per portion: Energy 231kcal/971kJ; Protein 3.7g; Carbohydrate 31.2g, of which sugars 14.5g; Fat 11g, of which saturates 6.4g; Cholesterol 70mg; Calcium 94mg; Fibre 11g; Sodium 16.8g.

Pear and polenta cake

Polenta gives the light sponge surrounding sliced pears a nutty corn flavour that complements the fruit perfectly. Serve as a dessert with custard or cream.

SERVES 10

175g/6oz/³⁄₄ cup golden caster
   (superfine) sugar

4 ripe pears

juice of ¹⁄₂ lemon

30ml/2 tbsp clear honey

3 eggs

seeds from 1 vanilla pod

120ml/4fl oz/¹⁄₂ cup sunflower oil

115g/4oz/1 cup self-raising
   (self-rising) flour

50g/2oz/¹⁄₃ cup instant polenta

COOK'S TIP

Use the tip of a small, sharp knife to scrape out the vanilla seeds. If you do not have a vanilla pod, use 5ml/1 tsp vanilla extract instead.

1 Preheat the oven to 180°C/350°F/Gas 4. Generously grease and line a 21cm/8¹⁄₂in round cake tin (pan). Sprinkle 30ml/2 tbsp of the golden caster sugar over the base of the prepared tin.

2 Peel and core the pears. Cut into chunky slices and toss them in the lemon juice. Arrange them on the base of the prepared cake tin. Drizzle the honey over the pears and set aside.

3 Mix together the eggs, seeds from the vanilla pod and the remaining golden caster sugar in a bowl. Beat until thick and creamy, then gradually beat in the oil. Sift together the flour and polenta and fold into the egg mixture.

4 Pour the mixture carefully into the tin over the pears. Bake for about 50 minutes or until a skewer inserted into the centre comes out clean. Cool in the tin for 10 minutes, then turn the cake out on to a plate, peel off the lining paper, invert and slice.

Nutritional information per portion: Energy 256kcal/1077kJ; Protein 3.7g; Carbohydrate 38.9g, of which sugars 26.7g; Fat 10.5g, of which saturates 1.5g; Cholesterol 57mg; Calcium 65mg; Fibre 1.8g; Sodium 66mg.

Pine nut and almond cake

This unusual recipe uses olive oil, toasted semolina and nuts to give the cake a rich flavour and a dense, grainy texture. Unlike traditional cakes it is not baked in the oven, but cooked in a pan.

SERVES 6–8

500g/1¼lb/2¾ cups caster (superfine) sugar
1 cinnamon stick
250ml/8fl oz/1 cup olive oil
350g/12oz/2 cups coarse semolina
50g/2oz/½ cup blanched almonds
30ml/2 tbsp pine nuts
5ml/1 tsp ground cinnamon

1 Put the sugar in a heavy pan with 1 litre/1¾ pints/4 cups cold water and the cinnamon stick. Bring to the boil, stirring until the sugar dissolves, then boil without stirring for 4 minutes to make a syrup.

2 Meanwhile, heat the oil in a separate, heavy pan. When it is almost smoking, add the semolina gradually and stir constantly until it turns light brown. Lower the heat, add the almonds and pine nuts, and brown for 2–3 minutes, stirring.

3 Take the semolina mixture off the heat and set aside. Remove the cinnamon stick from the hot syrup using a slotted spoon and discard it. Carefully add the hot syrup to the semolina mixture, stirring all the time. The mixture will hiss and spit at this point, so stand well away from it. Return the pan to a gentle heat and stir until the syrup has been absorbed and the mixture is smooth.

4 Remove the pan from the heat, cover it with a clean dish towel and leave it to stand for 10 minutes so that any remaining moisture is absorbed. Spoon the mixture into a 20–23cm/8–9in round non-stick cake tin (pan), and leave to cool. When cold, turn it on out to a platter and dust it with the cinnamon.

Nutritional information per portion: Energy 643kcal/2706kJ; Protein 6.8g; Carbohydrate 99.8g, of which sugars 65.7g; Fat 26.8g, of which saturates 3.3g; Cholesterol 0mg; Calcium 56mg; Fibre 1.5g; Sodium 10mg.

Yogurt cake with pistachio nuts

Flavoured with vanilla seeds and pistachio nuts, this unusual cake contains very little flour.
The texture is lightened with whisked egg whites. Serve it with passion fruit for a summer dessert.

SERVES 8–12

3 eggs, separated
75g/3oz/scant 1/2 cup caster
    (superfine) sugar
seeds from 2 vanilla pods (beans)
300ml/1/2 pint/11/4 cups Greek
    (US strained plain) yogurt
grated rind and juice of 1 lemon
15ml/1 tbsp plain (all-purpose) flour
a handful of pistachio nuts,
    roughly chopped
4–6 fresh passion fruit, to serve
90ml/6 tbsp crème fraîche,
    to serve (optional)

1 Preheat the oven to 180°C/350°F/Gas 4. Grease and line a 25cm/10in square shallow tin (pan) with baking parchment.

2 In a mixing bowl, beat the egg yolks with 50g/2oz/1/4 cup sugar until pale and fluffy. Beat in the vanilla seeds and stir in the yogurt, lemon rind and juice. Sift in the flour and beat well until light and airy.

3 Put the egg whites into a clean, grease-free bowl and whisk until they form stiff peaks, then gradually whisk in the rest of the sugar to form soft peaks.

4 Fold the whisked whites into the yogurt mixture. Turn the batter into the cake tin. Put the tin in a roasting pan and pour water in the pan to come halfway up the cake tin. Bake for 20 minutes, or until risen and just set.

5 Sprinkle the nuts over the cake and bake for another 20 minutes. Serve warm or cold with passion fruit and crème fraîche, if you like.

Nutritional information per portion: Energy 152kcal/638kJ; Protein 6.6g; Carbohydrate 16g, of which sugars 14.1g; Fat 7.9g, of which saturates 3.4g; Cholesterol 95mg; Calcium 99mg; Fibre 0.1g; Sodium 71mg.

Walnut cake

Brandy, orange and cinnamon warmed in a sugar syrup are poured over this rich cake, making it superbly moist and full of complementary flavours.

SERVES 10–12

150g/5oz/10 tbsp unsalted butter,
    plus extra for greasing
115g/4oz/generous ½ cup caster
    (superfine) sugar
4 eggs, separated
60ml/4 tbsp brandy
2.5ml/½ tsp ground cinnamon
300g/11oz/2¾ cups walnuts,
    coarsely chopped
150g/5oz/1¼ cups self-raising
    (self-rising) flour
5ml/1 tsp baking powder
a pinch of salt

FOR THE SYRUP

250g/9oz/1¼ cups caster
    (superfine) sugar
30ml/2 tbsp brandy
2 or 3 strips of pared orange rind
2 cinnamon sticks

1 Preheat the oven to 190°C/375°F/ Gas 5. Grease and line a 35 x 23cm/ 14 x 9in shallow cake tin (pan).

2 In a bowl, beat the butter and sugar together until light and fluffy. Beat in the egg yolks one at a time. Stir in the brandy and cinnamon, and then stir in the chopped walnuts.

3 Sift the flour and baking powder and set aside. Put the egg whites and salt into a clean, grease-free bowl and whisk to form stiff peaks. Gradually fold in the butter and sugar mixture, alternating with the flour. Spread the batter evenly in the tin.

4 Bake for 40 minutes. Meanwhile, make the syrup. Mix the sugar and 300ml/½ pint/1¼ cups water in a small pan. Heat gently, stirring, until the sugar has dissolved. Bring to the boil, lower the heat and add the brandy, orange rind and cinnamon sticks. Simmer for 10 minutes.

5 The cake is cooked when the top is golden and a skewer inserted into the centre comes out clean. Set on a wire rack in the tin. Remove the lining and slice the cake into diamonds while hot. Strain the syrup over it. Leave for 10–20 minutes. Turn out on to a wire rack. Serve cold.

Nutritional information per portion: Energy 563kcal/2349kJ; Protein 8.5g; Carbohydrate 50.6g, of which sugars 39.2g; Fat 35.3g, of which saturates 10.1g; Cholesterol 108mg; Calcium 114mg; Fibre 1.5g; Sodium 177mg.

Frosted carrot and parsnip cake

The carrots and parsnips in this deliciously light and crumbly cake help to keep it moist. The creamy sweetness of the cooked meringue topping contrasts with the cake's light crumb.

SERVES 8

grated rind of 1 lemon
grated rind and juice of 1 orange
15ml/1 tbsp caster (superfine) sugar
225g/8oz/1 cup butter
225g/8oz/1 cup soft light brown sugar
4 eggs
225g/8oz/1²⁄₃ cups mixed carrots
   and parsnips, grated
115g/4oz/1¹⁄₄ cups sultanas
   (golden raisins)
225g/8oz/2 cups self-raising (self-rising)
   wholemeal (whole-wheat) flour, sifted
   with 5ml/1 tsp baking powder

FOR THE TOPPING

50g/2oz/¹⁄₄ cup caster (superfine) sugar
1 egg white
a pinch of salt

1 Preheat the oven to 180°C/350°F/ Gas 4. Lightly grease a 20cm/8in loose-based cake tin (pan) and line the base with baking parchment.

2 Put half the lemon and orange rind in a bowl and mix with the caster sugar. Arrange the sugar-coated rind on baking parchment and leave to dry.

3 Cream the butter and sugar, then beat in the eggs. Stir in the unsugared rinds, grated carrots and parsnips, sultanas and 30ml/2 tbsp orange juice. Gradually fold in the flour and baking powder, and put into the tin.

4 Bake for 1¹⁄₂ hours until golden and just firm. Leave to cool slightly in the tin, then turn out on to a plate to cool.

5 For the topping, place the sugar in a bowl over boiling water with 30ml/ 2 tbsp of the orange juice. Stir over the heat until the sugar dissolves. Off the heat, add the egg white and salt, and whisk for 1 minute. Return to the heat and whisk for 6 minutes until stiff and glossy. Allow to cool slightly.

6 Swirl the topping over the cake and leave to firm up for 1 hour. Sprinkle with the sugared rind to decorate.

Nutritional information per portion: Energy 414kcal/1734kJ; Protein 6.2g; Carbohydrate 52.8g, of which sugars 38.9g; Fat 21.3g, of which saturates 12.4g; Cholesterol 124mg; Calcium 47mg; Fibre 2.3g; Sodium 175mg.

Pineapple and ginger upside-down cake

This light and moist cake has a sticky ginger glaze over stem ginger and pineapple pieces, which are arranged in the cake tin before the cake batter is added. It is superb served warm.

SERVES 8

20g/¾oz/1½ tbsp butter

2 pieces preserved stem ginger, chopped, plus 60ml/4 tbsp syrup

450g/1lb can pineapple pieces in natural juice, drained

250g/9oz/2¼ cups self-raising (self-rising) wholemeal (whole-wheat) flour

15ml/1 tbsp baking powder

5ml/1 tsp ground ginger

5ml/1 tsp ground cinnamon

115g/4oz/½ cup soft light brown sugar

250ml/8fl oz/1 cup full cream (whole) milk

45ml/3 tbsp sunflower oil

1 banana, peeled

1 Preheat the oven to 180°C/235°F/ Gas 4. Grease and line a 20cm/8in round deep cake tin (pan). Melt the butter in a pan over a gentle heat, then stir in the ginger syrup. Turn up the heat and stir until it thickens.

2 Pour the mixture into the tin and smooth out to the sides. Arrange the stem ginger and one-third of the pineapple pieces in the syrup in the tin. Set aside.

3 Sift together the flour, baking powder and spices into a large bowl, then stir in the sugar.

4 In a food processor or blender, blend together the milk, oil, the remaining pineapple and the banana until almost smooth, then add to the flour. Stir until combined.

5 Spoon the mixture over the pineapple and ginger pieces in the tin and smooth level.

6 Bake for 45 minutes, or until a skewer inserted into the centre of the cake comes out clean. Leave to cool slightly, then place a serving plate over the tin and turn upside down. Remove the lining.

Nutritional information per portion: Energy 358kcal/1508kJ; Protein 4.6g; Carbohydrate 55.2g, of which sugars 47.1g; Fat 14.8g, of which saturates 8.3g; Cholesterol 126mg; Calcium 63mg; Fibre 1g; Sodium 126mg.

Griestorte with pineapple filling

This classic European gateau uses semolina and ground almonds to give it a delicious crunchy texture. The filling of cream, pineapple and chocolate makes a soft, tangy contrast to the cake.

SERVES 8

3 eggs, separated
115g/4oz/generous ½ cup caster (superfine) sugar
finely grated rind and juice of ½ lemon
30ml/2 tbsp ground almonds
50g/2oz/⅓ cup fine semolina
icing (confectioners') sugar, for dusting
chocolate curls or flakes, to decorate

FOR THE FILLING

300ml/½ pint/1¼ cups double (heavy) cream
4 slices canned pineapple, drained and chopped
75g/3oz dark (bittersweet) chocolate, coarsely grated

1 Preheat the oven to 180°C/350°F/Gas 4. Grease and line a 20cm/8in round deep cake tin (pan) with baking parchment. Whisk the egg yolks with the sugar and lemon rind until pale and light. Add the lemon juice. Whisk until thick and the mixture leaves a ribbon trail when the whisk is lifted. Fold in the almonds and semolina.

2 Put the egg whites into a clean, grease-free bowl and whisk to form soft peaks. Fold into the yolk mixture.

3 Spoon into the tin and bake for 30–35 minutes, or until risen and pale golden. Cool in the tin for 5 minutes. Turn the cake out on to a wire rack and cool. Remove the papers. Cut the cake in half horizontally.

4 Whip the cream until it holds its shape, then fold in the pineapple and chocolate. Use the cream to sandwich the cakes together, dust the top with icing sugar, then decorate with chocolate curls.

Nutritional information per portion: Energy 356kcal/1484kJ; Protein 5g; Carbohydrate 29.7g, of which sugars 24.2g; Fat 27.2g, of which saturates 13.6g; Cholesterol 121mg; Calcium 52mg; Fibre 0.5g; Sodium 44mg.

Layer cake with cream and raspberries

This lovely cake has a custard layer as well as a raspberry layer, and a rich cream topping. For the best flavour and texture, bake the cake a day before assembling it.

SERVES 10–12

FOR THE CAKE
115g/4oz/1/2 cup unsalted butter
200g/7oz/1 cup caster (superfine) sugar
4 eggs, separated
45ml/3 tbsp full cream (whole) milk
175g/6oz/11/2 cups plain (all-purpose) flour
25ml/11/2 tbsp cornflour (cornstarch)
7.5ml/11/2 tsp baking powder
1.5ml/1/4 tsp salt
5ml/1 tsp vanilla sugar
fresh raspberries, to decorate

FOR THE RASPBERRY FILLING
375g/13oz/3 cups raspberries, crushed in a bowl,
    with sugar to taste

FOR THE CUSTARD FILLING
2 eggs
90g/31/2oz/1/2 cup caster (superfine) sugar
15ml/1 tbsp potato flour or cornflour (cornstarch)
350ml/12fl oz/11/2 cups full cream (whole) milk
a pinch of salt

FOR THE CREAM TOPPING
475ml/16fl oz/2 cups double (heavy) cream
    or whipping cream
25g/1oz/1/4 cup icing (confectioners') sugar
5ml/1 tsp vanilla sugar

1 Grease and flour three 23cm/9in layer cake tins (pans). Preheat the oven to 230°C/450°F/Gas 8. Cream the butter with the sugar. Beat in the egg yolks, one at a time. Stir in the milk until blended. In a separate bowl, sift the flour, cornflour, baking powder, salt and vanilla sugar. Fold into the egg mixture.

2 Whisk the egg whites in a separate bowl until stiff peaks form. Gently fold the egg whites into the cake mixture. Divide evenly among the tins and smooth to the edges. Bake for 12 minutes. Leave to cool for 10 minutes, then remove from the tins and cool on a rack.

3 For the custard, whisk the eggs and sugar in a pan until blended. Whisk in the potato flour or cornflour and milk. Add the salt. Stir over a low heat for 6 minutes, until thickened. Remove from the heat and cool. Beat the cream until soft peaks form. Stir in the icing sugar and vanilla sugar, then beat until stiff.

4 To assemble the cake, invert one layer on a plate and spread with the raspberry filling. Add a second cake and spread with the custard. Top with the last cake. Spread whipped cream over the sides and top of the cake. Chill until ready to serve, then decorate with raspberries.

Nutritional information per portion: Energy 433kcal/1811kJ; Protein 6.1g; Carbohydrate 44.6g, of which sugars 30.4g; Fat 27g, of which saturates 15.9g; Cholesterol 157mg; Calcium 86mg; Fibre 1.2g; Sodium 109mg.

Summer celebration shortcake

This crisp dessert contains crunchy almonds, which go particularly well with the strawberries and cream filling. The top layer is divided into portions, giving it an attractive appearance as well.

SERVES 8

175g/6oz/¾ cup butter, plus extra
    for greasing
150g/5oz/1¼ cups plain
    (all-purpose) flour
115g/4oz/1 cup ground almonds
50g/2oz/¼ cup caster (superfine) sugar
25g/1oz/¼ cup flaked (sliced) almonds

FOR THE FILLING AND DECORATION

300ml/½ pint/1¼ cups double
    (heavy) cream
450g/1lb/4 cups fresh strawberries,
    hulled and chopped, plus 9 whole
15ml/1 tbsp amaretto (optional)
icing (confectioners') sugar, for dusting

1 Preheat the oven to 180°C/350°F/Gas 4. Grease two baking sheets. Rub the butter into the flour until it forms fine crumbs, then stir in the ground almonds and sugar. Mix to a soft dough and knead until smooth.

2 Roll half of the dough into a 20cm/8in round and cut out neatly. Put on a baking sheet and sprinkle over half the almonds. Roll out the rest of the dough to make a second round. Sprinkle over the remaining almonds. Prick each with a fork. Bake for 20 minutes, or until pale golden. While still warm, mark one into eight triangles and leave to cool. Cut the triangles when cold.

3 Whip the cream until it forms soft peaks. Place a quarter in a piping (pastry) bag fitted with a star nozzle. Fold the chopped strawberries into the remaining cream with the liqueur, if using. Put the whole shortbread on a plate. Pile the fruit filling on top and arrange the eight triangles on top.

4 Pipe a cream rosette on each one and top with a strawberry, then put the last strawberry in the centre. Dust lightly with icing sugar. Serve immediately.

Nutritional information per portion: Energy 364kcal/1515kJ; Protein 4.3g; Carbohydrate 29.9g, of which sugars 8.5g; Fat 25.6g, of which saturates 15.6g; Cholesterol 87mg; Calcium 70mg; Fibre 1.2g; Sodium 76mg.

Swiss roll

Rolled sponge cakes are easy to make and versatile. They can be filled with delectable fillings that range from fresh fruit to buttercream. This one has chocolate buttercream inside.

SERVES 12

50g/2oz/¹/₂ cup self-raising (self-rising) flour

25g/1oz/¹/₄ cup cornflour (cornstarch)

5ml/1 tsp baking powder

3 eggs

250g/9oz/1¹/₄ cups caster (superfine) sugar

30ml/2 tbsp water

FOR THE CHOCOLATE BUTTERCREAM FILLING

50g/2oz/¹/₄ cup unsalted butter

90g/3oz/²/₃ cup icing (confectioners') sugar, sifted

1 egg yolk

30ml/2 tbsp unsweetened cocoa powder, sifted, plus extra for dusting

1 Preheat the oven to 190°C/375°F/Gas 5. Lightly grease a 27 x 38cm/10¹/₂ x 15in Swiss roll tin (jelly roll pan). Line with baking parchment and lightly grease.

2 Sift the flour, cornflour and baking powder into a bowl. Whisk the eggs and 150g/5oz/³/₄ cup of the sugar in a separate bowl until light and foamy. Gradually fold the flour into the egg mixture, then beat until smooth. Add the water. Spread the batter evenly in the tin and bake for 10–12 minutes until golden brown. Sprinkle a clean dish towel with the remaining sugar.

3 To make the filling, cream the butter and icing sugar until light and fluffy. Stir in the egg yolk until well blended, add the cocoa and blend.

4 Turn the cake out on to the prepared towel, remove the parchment, and trim the edges. While warm, roll the cake up with the towel inside. When cool, unroll it, spread with buttercream and roll up again, without the towel. Serve.

Nutritional information per portion: Energy 196kcal/826kJ; Protein 2.8g; Carbohydrate 35.1g, of which sugars 29.7g; Fat 5.9g, of which saturates 3g; Cholesterol 73mg; Calcium 34mg; Fibre 0.4g; Sodium 70mg.

Lemon roulade with lemon-curd cream

This feather-light roulade is flavoured with almonds and filled with a rich lemon-curd cream.
Use best-quality lemon curd for that perfect touch. Eat this cake fresh for the best taste.

SERVES 8

butter, for greasing
4 eggs, separated
115g/4oz/generous ½ cup caster
   (superfine) sugar
finely grated rind of 2 lemons
5ml/1 tsp vanilla extract
40g/1½ oz/⅓ cup plain
   (all-purpose) flour
25g/1oz/¼ cup ground almonds

FOR THE LEMON CREAM

300ml/½ pint/1¼ cups double
   (heavy) cream
60ml/4 tbsp lemon curd
45ml/3 tbsp icing (confectioners')
   sugar, for dusting

1 Preheat the oven to 190°C/375°F/Gas 5. Grease and line a 33 x 23cm/ 13 x 9in Swiss roll tin (jelly roll pan) with baking parchment. Beat the egg yolks with half the sugar until foamy. Beat in the lemon rind and vanilla extract. Sift the flour over the egg mixture and fold in with the ground almonds.

2 Whisk the egg whites in a clean, grease-free bowl until stiff, glossy peaks form. Gradually whisk in the remaining sugar to form a stiff meringue. Stir half the meringue mixture into the egg yolk mixture, then, when combined, fold in the remainder of the mixture.

3 Pour the batter into the prepared tin and smooth level. Bake for 10 minutes, or until risen and spongy to the touch. Put the tin on a wire rack and cover loosely with a sheet of baking parchment and a damp dish towel. Leave to cool.

4 To make the lemon cream, whip the cream until it holds its shape, then fold in the lemon curd. Sift the icing sugar over a piece of baking parchment. Turn the sponge out on to it. Peel off the paper and spread over the lemon cream. Using the paper, roll up the sponge. Discard the paper and serve.

Nutritional information per portion: Energy 337kcal/1401kJ; Protein 5g; Carbohydrate 24.5g, of which sugars 18.9g; Fat 25.1g, of which saturates 13.6g; Cholesterol 148mg; Calcium 55mg; Fibre 0.4g; Sodium 50mg.

Chocolate roulade

If you can't get a block of creamed coconut, you could use desiccated (dry unsweetened shredded) coconut for the filling instead – it will still be rich and delicious.

SERVES 8

150g/5oz/³⁄₄ cup caster (superfine) sugar

5 eggs, separated

50g/2oz/¹⁄₂ cup unsweetened
    cocoa powder

FOR THE FILLING

300ml/¹⁄₂ pint/1¹⁄₄ cups double
    (heavy) cream

45ml/3 tbsp whisky

50g/2oz piece solid creamed coconut,
    finely grated

30ml/2 tbsp caster (superfine) sugar

FOR THE TOPPING

coarsely grated curls of fresh coconut

chocolate curls

1 Preheat the oven to 180°C/350°C/Gas 4. Grease a 32 x 23cm/13 x 9in Swiss roll tin (jelly roll pan) and line with baking parchment. Dust a large sheet of baking parchment with 30ml/2 tbsp of the sugar.

2 Put the egg yolks and remaining sugar in a heatproof bowl over simmering water, and whisk until thick enough to leave a trail. Sift in the cocoa, then fold in carefully. Whisk the egg whites in a grease-free bowl until they form soft peaks. Fold 15ml/1 tbsp of the whites into the chocolate mixture, then fold in the rest.

3 Scrape the mixture into the prepared tin. Smooth the surface with a metal spatula, then bake for 20–25 minutes or until well risen and springy to the touch. Turn out on to the sugar-dusted baking parchment and carefully peel off the lining paper. Cover with a damp dish towel and leave to cool.

4 Make the filling. Whisk the cream with the whisky until it just holds its shape, then stir in the creamed coconut and sugar. Uncover the sponge and spread three-quarters of the cream mixture to the edges. Roll up carefully from a long side. Transfer to a plate. Spoon the remaining cream mixture on top, then add the coconut curls and the chocolate curls.

Nutritional information per portion: Energy 394kcal/1640kJ; Protein 6.2g; Carbohydrate 25.3g, of which sugars 24.6g; Fat 29.3g, of which saturates 18g; Cholesterol 170mg; Calcium 58mg; Fibre 0.8g; Sodium 115mg.

Chocolate and almond cake

This rich, dense chocolate cake is filled with a sweet almond paste and coated in glossy dark chocolate icing. It is an indulgent dessert for a special occasion.

SERVES 6

6 eggs, separated
115g/4oz/generous ½ cup caster (superfine) sugar
150g/5oz/1¼ cups unsweetened cocoa powder
150g/5oz/1¼ cups ground almonds

FOR THE ALMOND PASTE
150g/5oz/¾ cups caster (superfine) sugar
120ml/4fl oz/½ cup water
150g/5oz/1¼ cups ground almonds
15–30ml/1–2 tbsp lemon juice, to taste
½ vanilla pod (bean)

FOR THE ICING
115g/4oz good quality dark (bittersweet)
   chocolate (minimum 70 per cent cocoa
   solids), chopped
25g/1oz/2 tbsp unsalted butter, cubed
120ml/4fl oz/½ cup double (heavy) cream
50g/2oz/½ cup icing (confectioners')
   sugar, sifted

1 Preheat the oven to 200°C/400°F/Gas 6. Grease and line a 20cm/8in springform cake tin (pan). Place the egg yolks in a large bowl and add the sugar. Beat together until the mixture is thick and creamy, then add the cocoa powder and ground almonds, and gently fold together.

2 Whisk the egg whites until stiff peaks form. Using a metal spoon, fold a tablespoonful of the egg whites into the egg yolk mixture, then fold in the rest. Spoon the mixture into the tin and bake for 1 hour, or until a skewer inserted into the centre comes out clean. Leave to cool completely in the tin.

3 To make the almond paste, put the sugar and water in a heavy pan, then heat gently until the sugar has completely dissolved. Bring to the boil and boil for 4–6 minutes, or until a thick syrup forms. Stir in the ground almonds and bring back to the boil. Transfer the paste to a bowl, then add the lemon juice. Split the vanilla pod in half and scrape the seeds into the bowl. Mix well to combine.

4 Remove the cake from the tin and carefully slice into two even layers. Spread the bottom half with the almond paste, then sandwich the second half on top.

5 To make the icing, melt the chocolate and butter in a heatproof bowl over a pan of simmering water. Remove from the heat and gently stir in the cream, then add the sifted icing sugar and stir to combine. Cover the top of the cake with the chocolate icing. Leave to set, then serve cut into slices.

Nutritional information per portion: Energy 892kcal/3726kJ; Protein 23g; Carbohydrate 73.7g, of which sugars 69.3g; Fat 58.4g, of which saturates 19g; Cholesterol 228mg; Calcium 226mg; Fibre 7.2g; Sodium 349mg.

Black Forest gateau

Famous all over the world, this cake hails from Germany. It's extremely decadent, full of chocolate, cream and Kirsch, but is a real dinner-party classic.

SERVES 12

100g/3½oz plain (semisweet) chocolate

100g/3½oz/7 tbsp butter, softened

100g/3½oz/½ cup caster (superfine) sugar

10ml/2 tsp vanilla extract or 20g/¾oz vanilla sugar

6 eggs, separated

a pinch of salt

100g/3½oz/¾ cup plain (all-purpose) flour

50g/2oz/½ cup cornflour (cornstarch)

5ml/1 tsp baking powder

FOR THE FILLING

500g/1¼lb bottled cherries

5 gelatine leaves, soaked in cold water for 5 minutes

750ml/1¼ pints/3 cups double (heavy) cream

5ml/1 tsp vanilla extract or 5g/⅛oz vanilla sugar

100ml/3½ fl oz/scant ½ cup Kirsch

TO DECORATE

12 glacé (candied) cherries

75g/3oz flaked chocolate

1 Break up the chocolate and melt it in a bowl over a pan of simmering water. Preheat the oven to 160°C/325°F/Gas 3. Butter a 30cm/12in cake tin (pan).

2 Cream the butter with the sugar and vanilla extract or vanilla sugar. Gradually beat in the egg yolks, until light and foamy. Mix in the melted chocolate. Beat the egg whites with a pinch of salt until stiff and fold them into the mixture. Sift the flour and cornflour with the baking powder and fold in. Turn the mixture into the prepared tin and bake for 45–60 minutes, until a skewer pushed into the centre comes out clean. Leave to cool a little in the tin, then take out and leave on a rack to cool completely.

3 Strain the juice from the cherries into a pan. Bring to the boil, remove from the heat and add the gelatine. Stir until the gelatine has dissolved. Leave to cool. Whip the cream with the vanilla until stiff.

4 Slice the cake into three layers. Sprinkle the bottom layer with half the Kirsch, then spread half of the cherry jelly over it and put half the cherries on top. Top with some cream. Put the second layer of cake on top, and repeat the layers of Kirsch, jelly, cherries and cream. Top with the final cake.

5 Spread cream around the sides of the cake, and pipe 12 whirls on the top. Add a glacé cherry to each. Sprinkle flaked chocolate on top of the cake and press the rest into the sides. Chill for 5 hours. Serve.

Nutritional information per portion: Energy 551kcal/2293kJ; Protein 5.7g; Carbohydrate 36.8g, of which sugars 26.2g; Fat 45.7g, of which saturates 25.5g; Cholesterol 196mg; Calcium 73mg; Fibre 0.5g; Sodium 128mg.

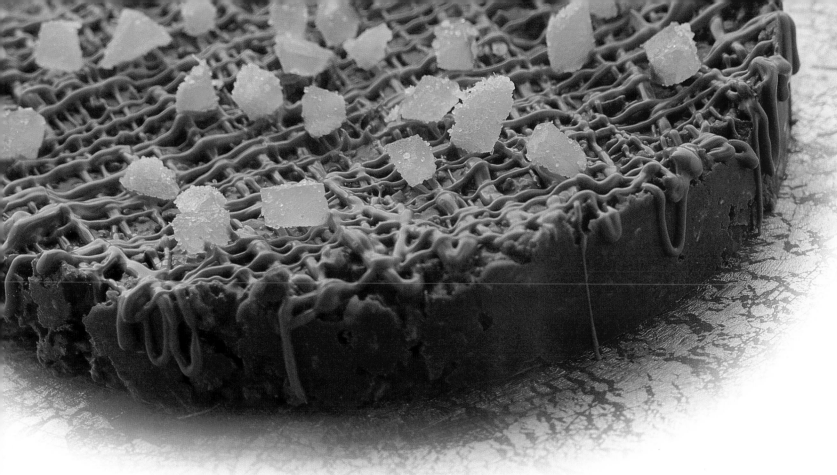

Chocolate ginger crunch cake

Ginger adds a flicker of fire to this delectable uncooked cake. Keep one in the refrigerator for spontaneous midnight feasts and other late-night treats.

SERVES 6

150g/5oz plain (semisweet) chocolate,
   broken into squares
50g/2oz/4 tbsp unsalted butter
115g/4oz ginger nut biscuits (gingersnaps)
4 pieces preserved stem ginger
30ml/2 tbsp stem ginger syrup
45ml/3 tbsp desiccated (dry unsweetened
   shredded) coconut

TO DECORATE
25g/1oz milk chocolate
pieces of crystallized ginger

1 Grease a 15cm/6in flan tin (pan); place it on a sheet of baking parchment. Melt the plain chocolate with the butter in a heatproof bowl over barely simmering water. Remove from the heat.

2 Crush the biscuits into small pieces with a rolling pin, then put them in a bowl.

3 Chop the stem ginger fairly finely and mix with the crushed ginger nut biscuits.

4 Stir the biscuit mixture, ginger syrup and coconut into the melted chocolate and butter, mixing well until evenly combined.

5 Turn the mixture into the prepared flan tin and press down firmly and evenly. Chill until set.

6 Remove the flan ring and paper and slide the cake on to a plate. Melt the milk chocolate, drizzle it over the top and decorate with the pieces of crystallized ginger.

Nutritional information per portion: Energy 298kcal/1251kJ; Protein 29.1g; Carbohydrate 18.5g, of which sugars 10.2g; Fat 12.5g, of which saturates 2.3g; Cholesterol 118mg; Calcium 48mg; Fibre 4.5g; Sodium 206mg.

Frosted chocolate fudge cake

Moist and dreamy, with an irresistibly rich and glossy chocolate fudge frosting, this cake couldn't be easier to make, and more wonderful to eat! Perfect for a special occasion.

SERVES 6–8

115g/4oz plain (semisweet) chocolate, broken into squares

175g/6oz/¾ cup unsalted butter or margarine, softened

200g/7oz/generous 1 cup light muscovado (brown) sugar

5ml/1 tsp vanilla extract

3 eggs, beaten

150ml/¼ pint/⅔ cup Greek (US strained plain) yogurt

150g/5oz/1¼ cups self-raising (self-rising) flour

icing (confectioners') sugar and chocolate curls, to decorate

FOR THE FROSTING

115g/4oz dark (bittersweet) chocolate, broken into squares

50g/2oz/4 tbsp unsalted butter

350g/12oz/3 cups icing (confectioners') sugar

90ml/6 tbsp Greek (US strained plain) yogurt

1 Preheat the oven to 190°C/375°F/Gas 5. Grease two 20cm/8in round sandwich cake tins (pans) and line the base of each tin with baking parchment.

2 Melt the chocolate gently in a heatproof bowl set over a pan of simmering water.

3 Cream the butter or margarine with the sugar until light and fluffy. Beat in the vanilla extract, then gradually add the beaten eggs, beating well after each addition. Stir in the melted chocolate and yogurt evenly. Fold in the flour with a metal spoon.

4 Divide the mixture between the tins. Bake for 30 minutes or until the cakes are firm to the touch. Turn out and cool on a wire rack.

5 For the frosting, melt the chocolate and butter in a pan over a low heat. Remove from the heat and stir in the icing sugar and yogurt.

6 Mix well, then beat until the frosting begins to cool and thicken slightly. Use a third of the frosting to sandwich the cakes together. Spread the remainder over the top and sides. Sprinkle with icing sugar and decorate with chocolate curls.

Nutritional information per portion: Energy 753kcal/3160kJ; Protein 8g; Carbohydrate 105.4g, of which sugars 90.9g; Fat 36.6g, of which saturates 21.7g; Cholesterol 133mg; Calcium 133mg; Fibre 1.3g; Sodium 224mg.

Raspberry and rose petal shortcakes

Rosewater-scented cream and fresh raspberries form the filling for this delectable dessert. Though they look impressive, these shortcakes are easy to make.

MAKES 6

115g/4oz/½ cup unsalted
    butter, softened
50g/2oz/¼ cup caster (superfine) sugar
½ vanilla pod (bean), split, seeds reserved
115g/4oz/1 cup plain (all-purpose) flour,
    plus extra for dusting
50g/2oz/⅓ cup semolina
icing (confectioners') sugar, for dusting

FOR THE FILLING

300ml/½ pint/1¼ cups double
    (heavy) cream
15ml/1 tbsp icing (confectioners') sugar
2.5ml/½ tsp rosewater
450g/1lb/4 cups raspberries

FOR THE DECORATION

12 miniature roses, unsprayed
6 mint sprigs
1 egg white, beaten
caster (superfine) sugar, for dusting

1 Cream the butter, caster sugar and vanilla seeds in a bowl until pale and fluffy. Sift the flour and semolina together, then gradually work the dry ingredients into the creamed mixture to make a firm dough.

2 Gently knead the dough on a floured surface until smooth. Roll out quite thinly and prick all over with a fork. Using a 7.5cm/3in fluted pastry (cookie) cutter, cut out 12 rounds. Place on a baking sheet and chill for 30 minutes.

3 Meanwhile, make the filling. Whisk the cream with the icing sugar until soft peaks form. Fold in the rosewater and chill until required.

4 Preheat the oven to 180°C/350°F/Gas 4. To make the decoration, paint the roses and leaves with the egg white. Dust with sugar; dry on a wire rack.

5 Bake the shortcakes for 15 minutes or until lightly golden. Lift them off the baking sheet with a fish slice or metal spatula and cool on a wire rack.

6 To assemble, spoon the rosewater cream on to half the biscuits. Add a layer of raspberries, then top with a second shortcake. Dust with icing sugar. Decorate with the frosted roses and mint sprigs.

Nutritional information per portion: Energy 544kcal/2271kJ; Protein 5g; Carbohydrate 36g, of which sugars 15g; Fat 43g, of which saturates 27g; Cholesterol 113mg; Calcium 75mg; Fibre 2.6g; Sodium 18mg.

Mini millefeuilles

This pâtisserie classic is a delectable combination of tender puff pastry sandwiched with luscious pastry cream. As it is difficult to cut, making individual servings is a brilliant solution.

SERVES 8

450g/1lb ready-made rough-puff or
    puff pastry
6 egg yolks
70g/2½oz/⅓ cup caster
    (superfine) sugar
45ml/3 tbsp plain (all-purpose) flour
350ml/12fl oz/1 ½ cups full cream
    (whole) milk
30ml/2 tbsp Kirsch or cherry
    liqueur (optional)
450g/1lb raspberries
icing (confectioners') sugar, for dusting
strawberry or raspberry coulis, to serve

1 Butter two baking sheets and sprinkle them very lightly with cold water. On a floured surface, roll out the pastry to a 3mm/⅛in thickness. Using a 10cm/4in pastry (cookie) cutter, cut out 12 rounds. Place on the baking sheets and prick with a fork. Chill for 30 minutes. Preheat the oven to 200°C/400°F/Gas 6.

2 Bake for about 15–20 minutes until golden. Transfer to wire racks to cool. Whisk the egg yolks and sugar until light and creamy, then whisk in the flour until just blended. Bring the milk to the boil over medium heat and pour it over the egg mixture, whisking. Return to the pan and boil for 2 minutes, whisking constantly. Remove the pan from the heat and whisk in the Kirsch or liqueur, if using. Pour into a bowl and press clear film (plastic wrap) on to the surface to prevent a skin forming. Set aside to cool.

3 Split the pastry rounds in half. Spread one round at a time with a little of the cream. Arrange a layer of raspberries on top. Top with a second pastry round. Spread with a little more cream and more raspberries. Top with a third pastry round flat side up. Dust with icing sugar. Serve with fruit coulis.

Nutritional information per portion: Energy 351kcal/1474kJ; Protein 8.2g; Carbohydrate 39.6g, of which sugars 15.2g; Fat 18.9g, of which saturates 1.7g; Cholesterol 154mg; Calcium 129mg; Fibre 1.6g; Sodium 203mg

Fresh berry Pavlova

Pavlova is the simplest of desserts, but it can also be the most stunning. You can fill it with any combination of berries, or sliced peaches and grapes.

SERVES 6–8

4 egg whites, at room temperature
225g/8oz/1 cup caster (superfine) sugar
5ml/1 tsp cornflour (cornstarch)
5ml/1 tsp cider vinegar
2.5ml/½ tsp pure vanilla extract
300ml/½ pint/1¼ cups double (heavy) cream
150ml/¼ pint/⅔ cup crème fraîche
350g/12oz/3 cups mixed berries
fresh mint sprigs, to decorate
icing (confectioners') sugar, for dusting

COOK'S TIP

Invert a plate on the baking parchment and draw round it with a pencil. Turn the paper over to avoid the pencil marking the meringue.

1 Preheat the oven to 140°C/275°F/Gas 1. Draw a circle on a piece of baking parchment (see Cook's Tip), turn it over and place on a baking sheet. Whisk the egg whites in a large grease-free bowl until they form stiff peaks. Gradually whisk in the sugar to make a stiff, glossy meringue. Sift the cornflour over and fold it in with the vinegar and vanilla.

2 Spoon the meringue mixture on to the paper-lined baking sheet, filling the marked circle. Swirl the top, and bake for 1¼ hours or until the meringue is crisp and very lightly golden. Switch off the oven, keeping the door closed, and allow the meringue to cool for 1–2 hours.

3 Carefully peel the paper from the meringue and transfer it to a serving plate. Whip the cream in a large mixing bowl until it forms soft peaks, fold in the crème fraîche, then spoon the mixture into the centre of the meringue case. Top with the berries and decorate with the mint sprigs. Sift icing sugar over the top and serve immediately.

Nutritional information per portion: Energy 394kcal/1639kJ; Protein 3g; Carbohydrate 35g, of which sugars 32g; Fat 28g, of which saturates 18g; Cholesterol 73mg; Calcium 40mg; Fibre 05g; Sodium 47mg.

Meringue mountain

A meringue can make an attractive centrepiece and is actually quite easy to make. Bake it ahead of time, if you like – it then takes just a few minutes to put together before serving.

SERVES 8–10

8 egg whites
450g/1lb/2¼ cups caster (superfine) sugar
pink food colouring

450ml/¾ pint/scant 2 cups double
 (heavy) cream
tiny rosebuds and candles, to decorate

1 Preheat the oven to 110°C/225°F/Gas ¼. Line three baking sheets with baking parchment. Rinse out the bowl of an electric mixer with boiling water, then dry completely.

2 Put the egg whites into the bowl of the mixer. Whisk the egg whites until they form soft peaks. Whisk in the sugar, 15ml/1 tbsp at a time, until the mixture forms stiff peaks.

3 Remove a quarter of the mixture and put it into a clean bowl. Colour it a pale pink with food colouring.

4 Spoon the pink meringue mixture into a piping (pastry) bag fitted with a star nozzle and pipe 15 pink rosettes on to one of the prepared baking sheets.

5 Spoon the remaining white mixture into a piping bag fitted with a star nozzle and pipe a thin 20cm/8in circle on to another of the baking sheets. Pipe about 15 small white rosettes with the remaining meringue on the third baking sheet.

6 Bake for 4 hours, swapping the trays from top to bottom halfway through. Turn off the heat and allow the meringues to dry out in the oven overnight if possible.

7 To assemble, whip the cream until it forms soft peaks, then spoon into a piping bag.

8 Put the circular base on a serving plate and pipe a cone shape of cream in the centre. Pipe a little cream on the base of each meringue rosette, then stick them on to form a conical shape. Decorate with rosebuds and candles, and serve immediately.

Nutritional information per portion: Energy 389kcal/1628kJ; Protein 3.3g; Carbohydrate 48.2g, of which sugars 48.2g; Fat 24.2g, of which saturates 13.5g; Cholesterol 59mg; Calcium 48mg; Fibre 0g; Sodium 68mg.

Croquembouche

This impressive tower is made from tiny, light-as-air choux buns filled with cream and delicately drizzled with caramel. It is served in France for special occasions and tastes wonderful.

SERVES 10

75g/3oz/6 tbsp unsalted butter, plus
 extra for greasing
115g/4oz/1 cup plain (all-purpose)
 flour, sifted
3 eggs

FOR THE FILLING
600ml/1 pint/2¼ cups double (heavy) cream
60ml/4 tbsp caster (superfine) sugar

FOR THE CARAMEL
115g/4oz/generous ½ cup caster (superfine) sugar

1 Preheat the oven to 200°C/400°F/Gas 6. Grease four baking sheets.

2 Melt the butter in a pan with 250ml/8fl oz/1 cup water and bring to the boil. Remove from the heat.

3 Sift the flour on to a paper sheet and pour into the pan all at once. Quickly beat together until the mixture forms a ball. Transfer to a bowl and whisk in the eggs, using an electric whisk, until a smooth, thick paste has formed.

4 Fill a piping (pastry) bag fitted with a 1cm/½in plain nozzle and pipe small balls about 2.5cm/1in wide on to the baking sheets, spacing them far apart.

5 Bake for 20 minutes, or until golden. Pierce a large hole in the base of each to release the steam, then return to the oven for a further 5 minutes. Cool on a wire rack.

6 To make the filling, whip the cream together with the 60ml/4 tbsp sugar, until it forms soft peaks.

7 Spoon into a piping bag fitted with a 5mm/¼in nozzle and pipe cream into each bun through the hole in the base. Arrange the buns in a pyramid.

8 To make the caramel, slowly heat the sugar in a pan until liquid. Drizzle the hot caramel over the pyramid, allowing it to run down over the buns, then serve immediately.

Nutritional information per portion: Energy 579kcal/2400kJ; Protein 6g; Carbohydrate 32.6g, of which sugars 24.4g; Fat 46.8g, of which saturates 28.3g; Cholesterol 159mg; Calcium 123mg; Fibre 0.3g; Sodium 138mg.

Chocolate profiteroles

These little golden puffs filled with simple vanilla ice cream cannot fail to impress. The ice-cream filling makes a delicious alternative to the usual whipped cream.

SERVES 4–6

110g/3¾oz/scant 1 cup plain
  (all-purpose) flour
1.5ml/¼ tsp salt
a pinch of freshly grated nutmeg
175ml/6fl oz/¾ cup water
75g/3oz/6 tbsp unsalted butter,
  cut into pieces

3 eggs
750ml/1¼ pints/3 cups vanilla ice cream

FOR THE CHOCOLATE SAUCE

275g/10oz plain (semisweet) chocolate,
  chopped into small pieces
120ml/4fl oz/½ cup warm water

1 Preheat the oven to 200°C/400°F/Gas 6. Grease a baking sheet. Sift the flour, salt and nutmeg on to a sheet of baking parchment or foil. For the sauce, melt the chocolate and water in a heatproof bowl set over a pan of simmering water. Stir until smooth. Keep warm.

2 Put the water and butter in a pan and bring to the boil. Remove from the heat and add the dry ingredients all at once. Beat with a wooden spoon for 1 minute until blended and the mixture starts to pull away from the pan. Set over a low heat and cook for 2 minutes, beating. Remove from the heat.

3 Beat 1 egg in a bowl and set aside. Add the remaining eggs, one at a time, to the flour mix, beating after each addition. Beat in just enough of the beaten egg to make a smooth, shiny dough. It should pull away and fall slowly when dropped from a spoon.

4 Using a tablespoon, ease the dough in 12 mounds on to the prepared baking sheet. Bake for 25–30 minutes, until the puffs are golden brown.

5 Remove the puffs from the oven and cut a small slit in the side of each of them to release the steam. Return the puffs to the oven, turn off the heat and leave them to dry out, with the door open.

6 Remove the ice cream from the freezer and allow it to soften for about 10 minutes. Split the profiteroles in half and put a small scoop of ice cream in each. Serve immediately, with the sauce.

Nutritional information per portion: Energy 647kcal/2707kJ; Protein 11.7g; Carbohydrate 68.2g, of which sugars 52.4g; Fat 36.9g, of which saturates 22.7g; Cholesterol 155mg; Calcium 182mg; Fibre 1.7g; Sodium 189mg.

Chocolate éclairs

Many of the éclairs sold in French cake shops are filled with crème pâtissière. Here, the crisp choux pastry fingers are filled with fresh cream, slightly sweetened and flavoured with vanilla.

SERVES 12

300ml/½ pint/1¼ cups double (heavy) cream
10ml/2 tsp icing (confectioners') sugar, sifted
1.5ml/¼ tsp vanilla extract
115g/4oz plain (semisweet) chocolate
30ml/2 tbsp water
25g/1oz/2 tbsp butter

FOR THE PASTRY
65g/2½oz/9 tbsp plain (all-purpose) flour
a pinch of salt
50g/2oz/¼ cup butter, diced
150ml/¼ pint/⅔ cup water
2 eggs, lightly beaten

1 Preheat the oven to 200°C/400°F/Gas 6. Grease a large baking sheet and line with baking parchment. To make the pastry, sift the flour and salt on to a small sheet of baking parchment. Heat the butter and water in a pan very gently until the butter melts. Increase the heat and bring to a rolling boil. Remove the pan from the heat and immediately add all the flour. Beat vigorously with a wooden spoon until the flour is mixed into the liquid.

2 Return the pan to low heat, then beat the mixture until it leaves the sides of the pan and forms a ball. Set the pan aside and allow to cool for 2–3 minutes. Add the beaten eggs, a little at a time, beating well after each addition, until you have a smooth, shiny paste, which is thick enough to hold its shape.

3 Spoon the choux pastry into a piping (pastry) bag fitted with a 2.5cm/1in plain nozzle. Pipe 10cm/4in lengths on to the prepared baking sheet. Use a wet knife to cut off the pastry at the nozzle.

4 Bake for 25–30 minutes, or until the pastries are well risen and golden brown. Remove from the oven and make a neat slit along the side of each to release the steam. Lower the oven temperature to 180°C/350°F/Gas 4 and bake for a further 5 minutes. Cool on a wire rack.

5 To make the filling, whip the cream with the icing sugar and vanilla extract until it just holds its shape. Spoon into a piping bag fitted with a 1cm/½in plain nozzle and use to fill the éclairs.

6 Place the chocolate and water in a small bowl set over a pan of hot water. Melt, stirring, until smooth. Remove from the heat and stir in the butter, until melted. Dip the top of each éclair in the melted chocolate, then place on a wire rack. Leave in a cool place until the chocolate is set. The éclairs are best served within 2 hours of being made, but they can be stored in the refrigerator for up to 24 hours.

Nutritional information per portion: Energy 253kcal/1050kJ; Protein 2.5g; Carbohydrate 11.6g, of which sugars 7.4g; Fat 22.2g, of which saturates 13.5g; Cholesterol 80mg; Calcium 29mg; Fibre 0.4g; Sodium 56mg.

Moroccan serpent cake

This is perhaps the most famous of all Moroccan pastries, filled with lightly fragrant almond paste, and dusted with icing sugar and cinnamon.

SERVES 8

8 sheets of filo pastry, thawed
    if frozen
50g/2oz/¼ cup butter, melted
1 egg, beaten
5ml/1 tsp ground cinnamon
icing (confectioners') sugar, for dusting

FOR THE ALMOND PASTE
50g/2oz/¼ cup butter, melted
225g/8oz/2 cups ground almonds
2.5ml/½ tsp almond extract
50g/2oz/½ cup icing
    (confectioners') sugar
1 egg yolk, beaten
15ml/1 tbsp rose water or orange
    flower water

1 To make the almond paste, mix the melted butter in a bowl with the ground almonds and almond extract. Add the sugar, egg yolk and rose or orange water, mix well and knead until pliable. Chill for 10 minutes.

2 Break the paste into ten even-sized balls and roll them into 10cm/4in sausages. Chill again. Preheat the oven to 180°C/350°F/Gas 4.

3 Overlap two sheets of filo to form a rectangle 18 x 56cm/7 x 22in. Secure the edges with butter, then brush butter all over. Cover with two more sheets and brush with butter.

4 Place five almond paste sausages along the lower edge of the filo sheet. Roll up tightly, tucking in the ends. Repeat to make two rolls. Shape the first into a loose coil. Transfer to a baking sheet brushed with butter. Attach the second and continue coiling into a snake. Tuck the end under.

5 Beat the egg with half the cinnamon. Brush over the pastry. Bake for 25 minutes. Invert the snake on to another baking sheet. Bake for 5–10 minutes more, until golden. Transfer to a plate and dust with icing sugar and the remaining cinnamon.

Nutritional information per portion: Energy 162kcal/675kJ; Protein 13.1g; Carbohydrate 8.5g, of which sugars 7g; Fat 8.6g, of which saturates 3.8g; Cholesterol 44mg; Calcium 42mg; Fibre 3g; Sodium 55mg.

Baklava

This famous Middle Eastern dessert is traditionally made with eight layers of pastry dough and seven layers of chopped nuts. The classic baklava uses just walnuts, but fillings vary.

SERVES 12

175g/6oz/¾ cup clarified or plain butter, or sunflower oil

100ml/3½fl oz/scant ½ cup sunflower oil

450g/1lb filo pastry sheets

450g/1lb walnuts, or a mixture of walnuts, pistachios and almonds, finely chopped

5ml/1 tsp ground cinnamon

FOR THE SYRUP

450g/1lb sugar

juice of 1 lemon, or 30ml/2 tbsp rose water

Nutritional information per portion: Energy 973kcal/4059kJ; Protein 12.2g; Carbohydrate 89.9g, of which sugars 60.9g; Fat 65.2g, of which saturates 15.6g; Cholesterol 47mg; Calcium 139mg; Fibre 3.1g; Sodium 141mg.

1 Preheat the oven to 160°C/325°F/Gas 3. Melt the butter and oil in a pan, then brush a little in a 30cm/12in square cake tin (pan). Place a sheet of filo in the bottom and brush it with butter and oil. Continue until you have used half the filo. Ease the sheets into the corners and trim the edges if they flop over the rim.

2 Spread the nuts over the buttered filo and sprinkle with the cinnamon, then continue as before with the remaining sheets. Brush the top one, then, using a sharp knife, cut diagonal parallel lines right through all the layers to form small diamonds. Cook in the oven for 1 hour, until golden.

3 Meanwhile, make the syrup. Put the sugar in a heavy pan, pour in 250ml/8fl oz/1 cup water and bring to the boil, stirring. When the sugar has dissolved, lower the heat and stir in the lemon juice or rose water, then simmer for about 15 minutes, until it thickens. Leave to cool in the pan.

4 When the baklava is ready, remove it from the oven and slowly pour the cooled syrup over the hot pastry. Return to the oven for 2–3 minutes, then leave to cool.

5 Once cool, lift the diamond-shaped pieces out of the tin and arrange them in a serving dish.

Apple strudel with vanilla sauce

*Originally from Austria, this dessert is now a classic throughout the world. The difficult part is
stretching the strudel dough until it is really thin. Use eating apples that have a tart, fruity flavour.*

SERVES 4

100g/3½ oz strong white bread flour,
  plus extra for dusting
5ml/1 tsp sunflower oil, plus extra for brushing
30–35ml/6–7 tsp lukewarm water
50g/2oz/4 tbsp butter, melted
icing (confectioners') sugar, to dust

FOR THE FILLING
10ml/2 tsp raisins
10ml/2 tsp brandy
400g/14oz eating apples, peeled and cored
juice of 1 lemon

5ml/1 tsp vanilla sugar or 2.5ml/½ tsp vanilla
  extract
100g/3½ oz caster (superfine) sugar
25g/1oz/¼ cup hazelnuts, finely chopped
50g/2oz/1 cup breadcrumbs

FOR THE VANILLA SAUCE
1 vanilla pod (bean)
200ml/7fl oz/scant 1 cup full cream (whole) milk
100ml/3½ fl oz/scant ½ cup single (light) cream
3 egg yolks
25g/1oz/2 tbsp caster (superfine) sugar

1 Mix the flour with the oil and water to make a smooth dough. Put it in an oiled bowl, cover and
leave for 30 minutes in a warm place. Line a baking tray with baking parchment.

2 To make the filling, soak the raisins in the brandy for 20 minutes. In the meantime, slice the apples
thinly, put them in a bowl and mix with the lemon juice. Add the vanilla sugar or extract, caster
sugar, chopped hazelnuts and breadcrumbs, and the soaked raisins and brandy.

3 Preheat the oven to 160°C/325°F/Gas 3. Spread a clean dish towel on the
work surface and dust it with flour. Roll out the dough on the towel, then
stretch it carefully on all sides using your hands, until it is the same size as
the towel. It should now be very thin.

4 Spoon the apple filling along the lower part of the dough, leaving a space
of 4cm/1½in on each side. Brush all the edges with melted butter.

5 Turn in the sides of the dough, then use the towel to help you roll up the
strudel around the filling. Brush with the rest of the melted butter and
transfer it carefully to the prepared baking tray.

6 Bake for 20–30 minutes, until the pastry is golden brown and crisp. Meanwhile, make the sauce.
Cut the vanilla pod in half lengthways and scrape out the seeds. Put the milk and cream in a pan
with the vanilla pod and seeds. Heat to boiling point, then remove from the heat.

7 Whisk the egg yolks with the sugar until light and thick, then whisk in the hot milk (having removed the vanilla pod). Set the bowl over a pan of simmering water and heat the sauce gently, stirring all the time, until it thickens. Make sure you do not overheat the mixture or the eggs will curdle.

8 When the strudel is cooked, remove it from the oven and leave it to cool for a few minutes. When ready to serve, dust the strudel with icing sugar. Serve warm, cut into slices, and accompanied by the vanilla sauce.

Nutritional information per portion: Energy 525kcal/2207kJ; Protein 8.9g; Carbohydrate 69.6g, of which sugars 41g; Fat 24.9g, of which saturates 11.6g; Cholesterol 195mg; Calcium 151mg; Fibre 3.1g; Sodium 228mg.

Fruit desserts

Whether fresh, baked, poached or deep-fried, fruits are remarkably versatile when it comes to making sumptuous desserts. When cooked, the sweet tastes of fruit are intensified and can be matched with complementary flavours, as in Baked Apples with Marzipan or Chocolate Amaretti Peaches. Fruit salads, however, can be equally delicious and are quick and easy to prepare – perfect for summer desserts that are light and healthy.

Honey and ginger baked apples

This sumptuous recipe for baked apples is a perfect winter dessert, featuring the warming flavours of ginger and honey, and served with a luxuriously creamy sauce.

SERVES 4

4 eating apples, such as Cox's Orange Pippin
    or Golden Delicious
30ml/2 tbsp finely chopped fresh root ginger
60ml/4 tbsp honey
25g/1oz/2 tbsp unsalted butter
60ml/4 tbsp medium white wine

FOR THE VANILLA SAUCE

300ml/½ pint/1¼ cups single
    (light) cream
1 vanilla pod (bean), split lengthways
2 egg yolks
30ml/2 tbsp caster (superfine) sugar

1 To make the vanilla sauce, put the cream and vanilla pod in a pan and heat gently to just below boiling point. Remove from the heat and leave to infuse for 10 minutes, then discard the vanilla pod.

2 Put the egg yolks and sugar in a bowl and whisk them together until pale and thick, then slowly pour in the cream in a steady stream, whisking all the time. Return the mixture to the pan and heat very gently, stirring, until the cream is thick enough to coat the back of a wooden spoon. (If you draw a finger horizontally across the back of the spoon, the sauce should be thick enough not to run down through the channel.)

3 Remove from the heat and leave to cool. Either stir from time to time or cover with a sheet of baking parchment to prevent a skin forming.

4 Preheat the oven to 160°C/325°F/Gas 3. Remove the cores from the apples leaving the stalk end intact, but remove the actual stalk. Fill each cavity with 2.5ml/½ tbsp chopped ginger and 15ml/1 tbsp honey.

5 Place the apples in an ovenproof dish, with the open end uppermost, and top each one with a piece of butter. Pour in the wine and bake in the oven, basting frequently with the cooking juices, for about 45 minutes, until the apples are tender. Serve the apples hot with the vanilla sauce.

VARIATION

Alternatively, you could serve the apples with sour cream or double (heavy) cream, if you prefer.

Nutritional information per portion: Energy 331kcal/1381kJ; Protein 4.3g; Carbohydrate 27.8g, of which sugars 27.8g; Fat 22.3g, of which saturates 13.2g; Cholesterol 155mg; Calcium 89mg; Fibre 1.2g; Sodium 68mg.

Baked apples with marzipan

This is a traditional recipe for the winter, when apples were once the only fresh fruits available and cooks needed to be really creative to find different ways to serve them.

SERVES 4

5ml/1 tsp raisins

10ml/2 tsp brandy

4 large, crisp eating apples,
    such as Braeburn

75g/3oz marzipan, chopped

juice of ½ lemon

20g/¾oz/¼ cup chopped
    pistachio nuts

vanilla sauce (see page 142) or double
    (heavy) cream, to serve

1 Preheat the oven to 160°C/325°F/ Gas 3. Soak the raisins in the brandy for 20 minutes.

2 Meanwhile, core the apples. Cut a small slice off the bottom of each one so that they will stand up. Score the skin around the apple in three places to prevent it rolling up during baking.

3 Mix the marzipan with the lemon juice, chopped pistachio nuts and raisins, and push the filling into the centre of the apples.

4 Put the apples on a baking tray lined with baking parchment, and bake for 20–25 minutes. Serve warm with vanilla sauce or cream.

Nutritional information per portion: Energy 150kcal/631kJ; Protein 2.2g; Carbohydrate 22.9g, of which sugars 22.7g; Fat 5.3g, of which saturates 0.6g; Cholesterol 0mg; Calcium 23mg; Fibre 2.3g; Sodium 33mg.

Chinese-style toffee apples

This classic dessert will make a great end to any meal. Wedges of crisp apple are encased in a light batter, then dipped in crispy caramel to make a sweet, sticky treat.

SERVES 4

115g/4oz/1 cup plain (all-purpose) flour
10ml/2 tsp baking powder
60ml/4 tbsp cornflour (cornstarch)
4 firm apples, peeled and cored
sunflower oil, for frying
200g/7oz/1 cup caster (superfine) sugar

1 In a mixing bowl, combine the flour, baking powder, cornflour and 175ml/6fl oz/³/₄ cup water. Stir to make a smooth batter and set aside.

2 Cut each apple into 8 thick wedges. Fill a wok one-third full of oil and heat to 180°C/350°F (or until a cube of bread, dropped into the oil, browns in 45 seconds).

3 In batches, dip the apple wedges in the batter, drain off any excess and deep-fry for 2 minutes, or until golden. Remove with a slotted spoon and drain on kitchen paper.

4 Reheat the oil to 180°C/350°F and re-fry the apple wedges for 2 minutes. Drain on kitchen paper and set aside.

5 Pour off all but 30ml/2 tbsp of the oil from the wok and stir in the sugar. Heat gently until the sugar melts and starts to caramelize. When it is light brown add the apple, a few pieces at a time, and toss to coat evenly.

6 Fill a large bowl with ice cubes and chilled water. Plunge the coated apple pieces briefly into the iced water to harden the caramel. Remove with a slotted spoon and serve.

Nutritional information per portion: Energy 390kcal/1655kJ; Protein 3g; Carbohydrate 87g, of which sugars 65g; Fat 5g, of which saturates 1g; Cholesterol 0mg; Calcium 72mg; Fibre 2.7g; Sodium 242mg.

Chocolate amaretti peaches

Guests are bound to be impressed when they are served these soft, sweet peaches filled to the brim with a fragrant mixture of amaretti, chocolate, orange, honey and cinnamon.

SERVES 4

115g/4oz amaretti, crushed
50g/2oz plain (semisweet)
   chocolate, chopped
grated rind of ½ orange
15ml/1 tbsp clear honey
1.5ml/¼ tsp ground cinnamon

1 egg white, lightly beaten
4 firm ripe peaches
150ml/¼ pint/⅔ cup white wine
15ml/1 tbsp caster (superfine) sugar
butter, for greasing
whipped cream, to serve

1 Preheat the oven to 190°C/375°F/Gas 5. Lightly grease a shallow ovenproof dish, which will just hold the peaches comfortably, with butter.

2 Mix together the crushed amaretti, chopped plain chocolate, orange rind, honey and cinnamon in a large bowl. Add the beaten egg white and mix to bind the mixture.

3 Halve and stone (pit) the peaches and fill the cavities with the chocolate mixture, mounding it up slightly. Arrange the stuffed peaches in the prepared ovenproof dish.

4 Mix the white wine and sugar in a jug (pitcher). Pour the wine mixture around the peaches.

5 Bake for 30–40 minutes until the peaches are tender when tested with a slim metal skewer and the filling is golden.

6 Serve the peaches immediately with a little of the cooking juices spooned over. Offer the whipped cream separately.

Nutritional information per portion: Energy 282kcal/1190kJ; Protein 4.1g; Carbohydrate 47g, of which sugars 34.4g; Fat 7.4g, of which saturates 3.8g; Cholesterol 1mg; Calcium 56mg; Fibre 2.4g; Sodium 117mg.

Poached pears in spiced red wine

Poached pears, like the ones in this recipe, date back to the 16th century. A beautiful deep, rich red colour, they always look attractive on the dinner table, and are surprisingly easy to make.

SERVES 4

2 firm ripe cooking pears, peeled and halved
500ml/17fl oz/generous 2 cups red wine
100g/3½ oz/½ cup sugar
pared rind of 1 orange
2 whole cloves
1 cinnamon stick
1 peppercorn
ice cream or whipped cream, to serve
4 mint sprigs, to decorate

COOK'S TIP

Use a skewer to check that the pears are cooked. They should be soft enough that the skewer slides in, but not so soft that they are in danger of breaking up. The cooking time required will depend on the variety of pear used, and their ripeness.

1 Scoop out the cores from the pears to leave a neat, round cavity. Put the pear halves in a shallow pan and pour over the wine to cover. Sprinkle with the sugar.

2 Pierce the strip of orange rind with the cloves. Add to the pan with the cinnamon stick and peppercorn. Bring to the boil, then reduce the heat, cover the pan and simmer for 30–45 minutes (see Cook's Tip).

3 Using a slotted spoon, lift the pears out and place them on a serving platter or in individual bowls. Increase the heat under the pan and boil the wine mixture for about 10 minutes until it has reduced by half and become syrupy.

4 Lift out and discard the orange rind, cinnamon stick and peppercorn. Spoon the syrup over the pears and leave to cool. Serve at room temperature or chill until required, periodically basting with the syrup so they develop a red hue.

5 Trim the base of each pear half if necessary so that it lies flat, with the cavity uppermost. Fill the cavities with ice cream or cream and decorate with mint.

Nutritional information per portion: Energy 378kcal/1595kJ; Protein 1g; Carbohydrate 65.7g, of which sugars 65.7g; Fat 0.2g, of which saturates 0g; Cholesterol 0mg; Calcium 53mg; Fibre 3.9g; Sodium 22mg.

Almond pears

This old-fashioned baked dessert is a tempting combination of cooked fruit and a sprinkling of ground almonds. The cream melts with the juices and ground almonds to form a delicious sauce.

SERVES 8

8 large ripe pears
juice of 1 lemon
25g/1oz/2 tbsp unsalted butter
350g/12oz/3 cups ground almonds
475ml/16fl oz/2 cups double
   (heavy) cream

1 Preheat the oven to 180°C/350°F/Gas 4. Peel and halve the pears and remove the cores. Put the pears into an ovenproof dish and sprinkle with lemon juice to stop them going brown.

2 Put a small piece of butter on each pear and sprinkle the ground almonds evenly over the top. Bake in the oven for about 15 minutes, basting once or twice with the juice, until they begin to soften.

3 Meanwhile, whisk the cream until it is beginning to hold its shape. When the pears are cooked, pour over the whipped cream and serve immediately.

Nutritional information per portion: Energy 607kcal/2511kJ; Protein 10.5g; Carbohydrate 15.3g, of which sugars 14.1g; Fat 56.4g, of which saturates 21.8g; Cholesterol 81mg; Calcium 147mg; Fibre 5.7g; Sodium 23mg.

Plum dumplings

These sweet dumplings, made with a potato dough, contain a whole plum, stuffed with cinnamon sugar. They are rich and satisfying, but may be best served after a light main course!

SERVES 4–6

675g/1½ lb potatoes, peeled
250ml/8fl oz/1 cup sour cream
75g/3oz/6 tbsp butter
2 eggs, beaten
250g/9oz/2¼ cups plain (all-purpose) flour,
    plus extra for dusting

8–12 plums
90g/3½ oz/¾ cup icing (confectioners') sugar
30ml/2 tbsp ground cinnamon
45ml/3 tbsp breadcrumbs
icing (confectioners') sugar and cinnamon,
    for dusting

1 Cut the potatoes into even-sized pieces and cook in a pan of lightly salted boiling water for 10–15 minutes, or until soft. Drain, leave to cool, then mash in a large bowl. Add the sour cream, 25g/1oz/2 tbsp butter, the eggs and flour to the mashed potato and stir to combine thoroughly.

2 Turn the dough out on to a lightly floured surface and knead lightly until the dough comes together and is firm. Add a little more flour if necessary – it should not be sticky.

3 Cut a slit down one side of each plum so that you can remove the stone (pit) while keeping the plum intact. Mix together the icing sugar and cinnamon, then push a teaspoonful into each of the plums.

4 Roll out the dough to about 5mm/¼ in thick and cut into eight or twelve 10cm/4in squares (depending on how many plums you have). Place a plum in the centre of each square, then bring up the dough and pinch the edges together to completely seal the plum in the dough.

5 Bring a large pan of water to the boil, and add the dumplings in batches of about six at a time. Cook for about 8 minutes, or until they rise to the surface. Remove with a slotted spoon, transfer to a bowl and keep warm while you cook the remaining dumplings.

6 Heat the remaining butter in a large frying pan, add the breadcrumbs and fry for a few minutes, until golden brown. Add the dumplings and gently turn in the breadcrumbs to coat. Transfer to a warm serving plate and dust with icing sugar and cinnamon. Serve immediately.

Nutritional information per portion: Energy 510kcal/2147kJ; Protein 11.1g; Carbohydrate 72.6g, of which sugars 18.6g; Fat 21.6g, of which saturates 12.4g; Cholesterol 115mg; Calcium 147mg; Fibre 5.3g; Sodium 190mg.

Oranges in hot coffee syrup

This recipe works well with most citrus fruits so you can experiment with the ingredients, if you like; try pink grapefruit or sweet, perfumed clementines, peeled but left whole.

SERVES 6

6 oranges
200g/7oz/1 cup sugar
50ml/2fl oz/¹/₄ cup cold water
100ml/3¹/₂fl oz/scant ¹/₂ cup boiling water
100ml/3¹/₂fl oz/scant ¹/₂ cup fresh strong brewed coffee
50g/2oz/¹/₂ cup pistachio nuts, chopped (optional)

1 Finely pare the rind from one orange; shred and reserve the rind. Peel the remaining oranges. Cut each one crossways into slices, then re-form with a cocktail stick (toothpick) through the centre.

2 Put the sugar and cold water in a heavy-based pan. Heat gently until the sugar dissolves, then bring to the boil and cook until the syrup turns pale gold.

3 Remove from the heat and carefully pour the boiling water into the pan. Return to the heat until the syrup has dissolved in the water. Stir in the coffee.

4 Add the oranges and the shredded rind to the coffee syrup. Simmer for 15–20 minutes, turning the oranges once during cooking. Sprinkle with pistachio nuts, if using, and serve the oranges hot in the syrup.

COOK'S TIP
Choose a pan in which the oranges will just fit in a single layer.

Nutritional information per portion: Energy 183kcal/782kJ; Protein 2g; Carbohydrate 46.4g, of which sugars 46.3g; Fat 0.1g, of which saturates 0g; Cholesterol 0mg; Calcium 84mg; Fibre 2.3g; Sodium 10mg.

Fresh fig compote

Lightly poaching figs in a vanilla and coffee syrup brings out their wonderful sweet flavour. Serve with some thick Greek yogurt, if you like.

SERVES 4–6

400ml/14fl oz/1²/₃ cups brewed coffee
115g/4oz/¹/₂ cup clear honey
1 vanilla pod (bean)
12 slightly under-ripe fresh figs
**Greek (US strained plain) yogurt,
    to serve (optional)**

COOK'S TIPS

• *Rinse and dry the vanilla pod; it can be used several times.*
• *Figs come in three main varieties – red, white and black – and all three are suitable for cooking. Naturally high in sugar, they are sweet and succulent and complement well the stronger flavours of coffee and vanilla.*

1 Choose a frying pan with a lid, large enough to hold the figs in a single layer. Pour in the coffee and add the honey.

2 Split the vanilla pod lengthways and scrape the seeds into the pan. Add the vanilla pod, then bring to the boil. Bring the syrup to a rapid boil and cook until reduced to about 175ml/6fl oz/³/₄ cup. Leave to cool.

3 Wash the figs and pierce the skins several times with a sharp skewer. Cut in half and add to the syrup. Lower the heat, cover and simmer for 5 minutes. Remove the figs from the syrup with a slotted spoon and set aside to cool.

4 Strain the syrup over the figs. Allow to stand for 1 hour before serving with yogurt, if you like.

Nutritional information per portion: Energy 147kcal/628kJ; Protein 1.7g; Carbohydrate 36g, of which sugars 35.8g; Fat 0.6g, of which saturates 0g; Cholesterol 0mg; Calcium 103mg; Fibre 3g; Sodium 27mg.

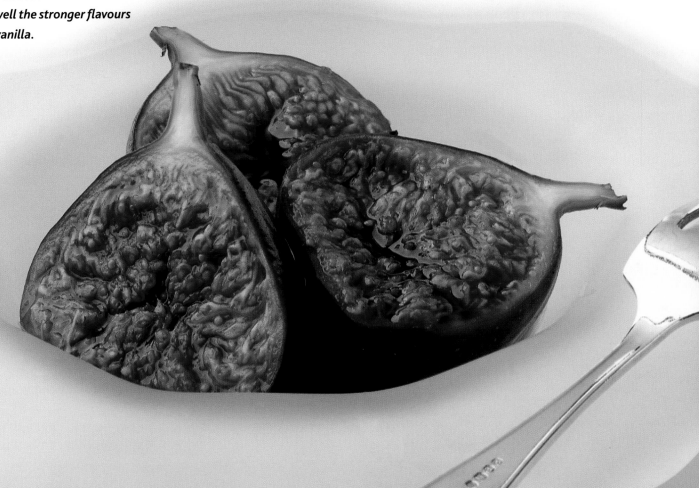

Caramelized pineapple in lemon grass syrup

*This stunning dessert, garnished with jewel-like pomegranate seeds, is superb for entertaining.
The tangy, zesty flavours of lemon grass and mint bring out the exquisite sweetness of the pineapple.*

SERVES 4

30ml/2 tbsp very finely chopped lemon grass,
   and 2 lemon grass stalks, halved lengthways
350g/12oz/1¾ cups caster
   (superfine) sugar
10ml/2 tsp chopped fresh mint leaves

2 small, ripe pineapples (approximately
   600g/1lb 5oz each)
15ml/1 tbsp sunflower oil
60ml/4 tbsp pomegranate seeds
crème fraîche, to serve (optional)

1 Place all of the lemon grass, 250g/9oz/1¼ cups of the caster sugar and the chopped mint leaves in a non-stick wok. Pour over 150ml/¼ pint/⅔ cup of water, place over a medium heat and bring to the boil.

2 Reduce the heat under the wok and simmer the mixture for 10–15 minutes, until thickened. Strain into a glass bowl, reserving the halved lemon grass stalks, then set aside.

3 Using a sharp knife, peel and core the pineapples, then cut them into 1cm/½in-thick slices. Sprinkle the slices with the remaining sugar.

4 Brush a large non-stick wok with the oil and place over a medium heat. Working in batches, cook the sugared pineapple slices for 4–5 minutes, on each side, until lightly caramelized.

5 Transfer the pineapple slices to a flat serving dish and sprinkle over the pomegranate seeds.

6 Pour the lemon grass syrup over the fruit and garnish with the reserved stalks. Serve with crème fraîche, if you like.

COOK'S TIP
To remove pomegranate seeds, halve the fruit and hold it over a bowl, cut side down. Tap all over with a wooden spoon and the seeds should drop out.

Nutritional information per portion: Energy 493kcal/2101kJ; Protein 1.6g; Carbohydrate 121.7g, of which sugars 121.7g; Fat 3.4g, of which saturates 0.3g; Cholesterol 0mg; Calcium 101mg; Fibre 3.6g; Sodium 11mg.

Banana fritters

You can find deep-fried banana fritters at food stalls and cafés throughout South-east Asia. This recipe is particularly delicious, as grated ginger and coconut are added to the batter.

SERVES 3–4

6–8 small or 3 large ripe bananas

corn or vegetable oil, for deep-frying

icing (confectioners') sugar or caster (superfine) sugar, for dusting

coconut cream, to serve

FOR THE BATTER

115g/4oz/1 cup plain (all-purpose) flour

5ml/1 tsp baking powder

a pinch of salt

2 eggs, lightly beaten

400g/14oz can coconut milk

15ml/1 tbsp palm sugar (jaggery)

25g/1oz fresh root ginger, finely grated

50g/2oz fresh coconut, grated, or desiccated (dry unsweetened shredded) coconut

TO FLAMBÉ (OPTIONAL)

15–30ml/1–2 tbsp sugar

rum

coconut cream

1 First make the batter. Sift the flour, baking powder and salt into a large bowl. Make a well in the centre and drop in the beaten eggs. Gradually pour in the coconut milk, beating until the batter is smooth. Beat in the sugar, grated ginger and coconut. Leave the batter to stand for 30 minutes.

2 Cut the banana in half, then cut each half lengthways. Beat the batter again, add the bananas and coat them well.

3 Heat the oil for deep-frying in a wok or deep pan. Working in batches and using a pair of tongs, fry the bananas until crisp and golden brown.

4 Lift them out and drain on kitchen paper. Dust with icing or caster sugar and serve warm, with coconut cream.

5 Alternatively, to flambé the banana fritters, arrange the deep-fried bananas in a wide, heavy pan and place over a medium heat. Sprinkle the sugar over the top and toss the bananas in the pan until they are sticky and slightly caramelized. Lower the heat, pour in the rum and set alight. (Have a lid handy to smother the flames if necessary.) Spoon the rum over the bananas until caramelized and serve immediately with coconut cream.

Nutritional information per portion: Energy 407kcal/1710kJ; Protein 7.8g; Carbohydrate 53.3g, of which sugars 29.7g; Fat 19.7g, of which saturates 8.8g; Cholesterol 95mg; Calcium 95mg; Fibre 3.4g; Sodium 151mg.

Baked bananas with hazelnut sauce

Bananas are completely transformed when baked in the oven, and the ice cream and sweet hazelnut sauce make this an even more luxurious yet simple dessert.

SERVES 4

4 large bananas
15ml/1 tbsp lemon juice
vanilla ice cream, to serve

FOR THE SAUCE
25g/1oz/2 tbsp unsalted butter
50g/2oz/¹⁄₂ cup hazelnuts, toasted and roughly chopped
45ml/3 tbsp golden (light corn) syrup
30ml/2 tbsp lemon juice

1 Preheat the oven to 180°C/350°F/ Gas 4. Place the unpeeled bananas on a baking sheet and brush them with the lemon juice. Bake for about 20 minutes, until the skins are turning black and the flesh gives a little when the bananas are gently squeezed.

2 To make the sauce, melt the butter in a small pan. Add the hazelnuts and cook gently for 1 minute.

3 Add the golden syrup and lemon juice and heat, stirring, for a further 1 minute. Set aside and keep warm.

4 Slit each banana open with a knife and open out the skins to reveal the tender flesh.

5 Transfer the bananas to serving plates and add scoops of ice cream. Pour the sauce over and serve.

Nutritional information per portion: Energy 382kcal/1598kJ; Protein 5.4g; Carbohydrate 49.4g, of which sugars 45.7g; Fat 18.6g, of which saturates 7.6g; Cholesterol 28mg; Calcium 88mg; Fibre 2.1g; Sodium 106mg.

Cantaloupe melon with grilled strawberries

If strawberries are slightly underripe, sprinkling them with a little sugar and then grilling them will help bring out their deliciously sweet flavour.

SERVES 4

115g/4oz/1 cup strawberries,
    hulled and halved
15ml/1 tbsp icing (confectioners') sugar,
    plus extra for dusting
½ cantaloupe melon

1 Preheat the grill (broiler) to high. Arrange the halved strawberries in a single layer, cut side up, on a baking sheet or in an ovenproof dish and dust with the icing sugar.

2 Grill (broil) the strawberries for 4–5 minutes, or until the sugar starts to bubble and turn golden.

3 Meanwhile, scoop out the seeds from the melon. Using a sharp knife, cut the melon into wedges, then remove the skin from each wedge.

4 Arrange the melon on a serving plate with the grilled strawberries. Serve immediately, dusted with a little extra icing sugar.

Nutritional information per portion: Energy 46kcal/197kJ; Protein 1g; Carbohydrate 10.9g, of which sugars 10.9g; Fat 0.2g, of which saturates 0g; Cholesterol 0mg; Calcium 32mg; Fibre 1.6g; Sodium 12mg.

Oranges with caramel wigs

This is a delicious way to turn simple fruit into something special. The slightly bitter, caramelized orange rind and syrup has a wonderful flavour and texture, and it looks elegant too.

SERVES 6

6 oranges
120g/4oz/generous ½ cup caster (superfine) sugar

1 Using a vegetable peeler, thinly pare 12 long strips of rind off the oranges. Peel all the oranges, reserving the rind and discarding the pith. Reserve the juice that has collected, then freeze the oranges separately for 30 minutes. Slice the oranges, reform and secure with a cocktail stick (toothpick). Chill.

2 Simmer the rind in boiling water for 5 minutes. Drain, rinse, and repeat. Cut into leaf shapes with scissors. Put half the sugar into a small pan with 15ml/ 1 tbsp water. Heat gently until it caramelizes, shaking the pan a little. As soon as it colours, dip the bottom of the pan into cold water. Add 30ml/2 tbsp hot water and the orange rind, then stir. Turn the rind on to a plate to cool.

3 Put the remaining sugar in a pan with 15ml/1 tbsp water, and make caramel as before. Once coloured, pour in 120ml/4fl oz/½ cup boiling water and stir to dissolve. Add the reserved juices. Arrange the rind on top of the oranges, remove the cocktail sticks, pour a little caramel round each orange and serve.

Nutritional information per portion: Energy 122kcal/521kJ; Protein 1.4g; Carbohydrate 30.8g, of which sugars 30.8g; Fat 0.1g, of which saturates 0g; Cholesterol 0mg; Calcium 66mg; Fibre 2g; Sodium 7mg.

Deep-fried cherries

Fresh fruit coated with a simple batter and then deep-fried is delicious and makes an unusual dessert. These succulent cherries are perfect served with a classic vanilla ice cream.

SERVES 4–6

450g/1lb ripe red cherries, on their stalks
225g/8oz packet batter mix (see Cook's Tip)
1 egg
vegetable oil, for deep-frying
vanilla ice cream, to serve (optional)

COOK'S TIP

To make your own batter, sift 115g/4oz/ 1 cup plain (all-purpose) flour and a pinch of salt into a bowl. Whisk in 1 egg and 150ml/¼ pint/⅔ cup milk. If you make your own batter, you do not need to add the extra egg in step 2.

1 Gently wash the cherries and pat dry with kitchen paper. Tie the stalks together with fine string to form clusters of four or five cherries.

2 Make up the batter mix according to the instructions on the packet, beating in the egg. Pour the vegetable oil into a deep-fat fryer or large, heavy pan and heat to 190°C/375°F.

3 Working in batches, half-dip each cherry cluster into the batter and then carefully drop the cluster into the hot oil. Fry for 3–4 minutes, or until golden. Remove the deep-fried cherries with a wire-mesh skimmer or slotted spoon and drain on a wire rack placed over crumpled kitchen paper. Serve immediately, with vanilla ice cream, if you like.

Nutritional information per portion: Energy 201kcal/840kJ; Protein 3.7g; Carbohydrate 25.7g, of which sugars 7.3g; Fat 10g, of which saturates 1.3g; Cholesterol 26mg; Calcium 46mg; Fibre 1.3g; Sodium 11mg.

Tropical scented red and orange fruit salad

This fresh fruit salad, with its special colour and exotic flavour, is a perfect dessert to serve after a rich, heavy meal. Make it a few hours ahead to let the flavours develop.

SERVES 4–6

350–400g/12–14oz/3–3½ cups
   strawberries, hulled and halved

3 oranges, peeled and segmented

3 small blood oranges, peeled
   and segmented

1–2 passion fruit

120ml/4fl oz/½ cup dry white wine

sugar, to taste

1 Put the strawberries and oranges into a serving bowl. Halve the passion fruit and spoon the flesh over the fruit.

2 Pour the white wine over the fruit and add sugar to taste. Toss gently, then chill the fruit salad until ready to serve.

VARIATION
Other fruits that can be added include pear, kiwi fruit and banana.

Nutritional information per portion: Energy 81kcal/342kJ; Protein 2g; Carbohydrate 15.6g, of which sugars 15.6g; Fat 0.2g, of which saturates 0g; Cholesterol 0mg; Calcium 75mg; Fibre 3g; Sodium 13mg.

Pistachio and rose water oranges

This light and citrussy dessert combines three Middle Eastern ingredients. It is delightfully fragrant and refreshing. If you don't have pistachio nuts, use hazelnuts instead.

SERVES 4

4 large oranges
30ml/2 tbsp rose water
30ml/2 tbsp shelled pistachio nuts,
    roughly chopped

COOK'S TIP
Rose-scented sugar is delicious sprinkled over fresh fruit salads. Wash and thoroughly dry a handful of rose petals and place in a sealed container filled with caster (superfine) sugar for 2–3 days. Remove the petals before using the sugar.

1 Slice the top and bottom off one of the oranges to expose the flesh. Using a small serrated knife, slice down between the pith and the flesh, working round the orange, to remove all the peel and pith.

2 Slice the orange into six rounds, reserving any juice. Repeat with the remaining oranges.

3 Arrange the orange rounds on a serving dish. Mix the reserved juice with the rose water and drizzle over the oranges. Cover the dish with clear film (plastic wrap) and chill for about 30 minutes.

4 When ready to serve, sprinkle the chopped pistachio nuts over the orange slices.

Nutritional information per portion: Energy 101kcal/424kJ; Protein 3g; Carbohydrate 13.4g, of which sugars 13.2g; Fat 4.3g, of which saturates 0.6g; Cholesterol 0mg; Calcium 79mg; Fibre 3g; Sodium 47mg.

Hot puddings

There is no better way to end a meal than with a steaming hot pudding, especially on a cold wintry evening when something substantial and warming is required. Try a classic dish like Crêpes Suzette or Hot Chocolate Soufflés for an elegant dinner-party dessert, or for a hearty and indulgent pudding, opt for Sticky Toffee Pudding or Plum Crumble. There are a few unusual flavours to try, too, such as Honey Pudding or Lingonberry and Semolina Pudding.

Crêpes Suzette

This is one of the best-known French desserts and is easy to make at home. You can make the crêpes in advance, then you will be able to put the dish together quickly at the last minute.

SERVES 6

120g/40z/²⁄₃ cup plain (all-purpose) flour
1.5ml/¹⁄₄ tsp salt
30g/1oz/2 tbsp caster (superfine) sugar
2 eggs, lightly beaten
250ml/8fl oz/1 cup milk
60ml/4 tbsp water
30ml/2 tbsp orange flower water or orange
    liqueur (optional)
30g/1oz/2 tbsp unsalted butter, melted,
    plus extra for frying

FOR THE ORANGE SAUCE

85g/3oz/6 tbsp unsalted butter
55g/2oz/¹⁄₄ cup caster (superfine) sugar
shredded rind and juice of 1 large orange
shredded rind and juice of 1 lemon
150ml/¹⁄₄ pint/²⁄₃ cup fresh orange juice
60ml/4 tbsp orange liqueur, plus extra for
    flaming (optional)
brandy, for flaming (optional)
orange segments, to decorate

1 In a medium bowl, sift together the flour, salt and sugar. Make a well in the centre and pour in the eggs. Using an electric whisk, beat the eggs, bringing in the flour gradually until it is all incorporated. Slowly whisk in the milk and water to make a smooth batter. Whisk in the orange flower water or liqueur, if using, then strain the batter into a large jug (pitcher) and set aside for 20–30 minutes. If the batter thickens, thin it with a little milk or water.

2 Heat an 18–20cm/7–8in crêpe pan (preferably non-stick) over a medium heat. Stir the melted butter into the crêpe batter. Brush the hot pan with a little extra melted butter and pour in about 30ml/2 tbsp of batter. Quickly tilt and rotate the pan to cover the base with a thin layer of batter. Cook for about 1 minute until the top is set and the base is golden.

3 With a palette knife or metal spatula, lift the edge to check the colour, then carefully turn over the crêpe and cook for 20–30 seconds. Turn on to a plate.

4 Continue cooking the crêpes, stirring the batter occasionally and brushing the pan with a little melted butter as and when necessary. Place a sheet of clear film (plastic wrap) between the crêpes as they are stacked to prevent sticking. (Crêpes can be prepared ahead to this point – wrap and chill until ready to use.)

5 To make the sauce, melt the butter in a large frying pan over a medium-low heat, then stir in the caster sugar, orange and lemon rind and juice, the additional fresh orange juice and the orange liqueur.

6 Place a crêpe in the pan browned-side down, swirling gently to coat with the sauce. Fold it in half, then in half again to form a triangle and push to the side of the pan. Continue heating and folding the crêpes until all are warm and covered with the sauce.

7 To flame the crêpes, heat 30–45ml/2–3 tbsp each of orange liqueur and brandy in a small pan over a medium heat. Remove the pan from the heat, carefully ignite the liquid with a match then gently pour over the crêpes. Serve immediately, decorated with the orange segments.

Nutritional information per portion: Energy 316kcal/1323kJ; Protein 5.6g; Carbohydrate 34.2g, of which sugars 19.6g; Fat 17.2g, of which saturates 10.1g; Cholesterol 103mg; Calcium 100mg; Fibre 0.6g; Sodium 152mg.

Apricot panettone pudding

The combination of light Italian fruited bread, apricots and pecan nuts produces a wonderfully rich version of traditional bread and butter pudding.

SERVES 6

350g/12oz panettone, sliced
into triangles
25g/1oz/¼ cup pecan nuts
75g/3oz/⅓ cup ready-to-eat dried
apricots, chopped
500ml/17fl oz/2¼ cups semi-skimmed
(low-fat) milk
5ml/1 tsp vanilla extract
1 large (US extra large) egg, beaten
30ml/2 tbsp maple syrup
2.5ml/½ tsp freshly grated nutmeg, plus
extra for sprinkling
demerara (raw) sugar, for sprinkling
cream, to serve (optional)

1 Grease a 1 litre/1¾ pint/4 cup baking dish. Arrange half the panettone in the base of the dish, sprinkle over half the pecan nuts and all the dried apricots, then add another layer of panettone on top, spreading it as evenly as you can.

2 Pour the milk into a small pan, add the vanilla extract, and warm over a medium heat until it just simmers.

3 In a bowl, mix together the beaten egg and maple syrup, grate in the nutmeg, then whisk in the hot milk.

4 Preheat the oven to 200°C/400°F/ Gas 6. Pour the milk mixture over the panettone, lightly pressing down each slice so that it is totally submerged in the mixture. Set the dish aside and leave the pudding to stand for at least 10 minutes.

5 Sprinkle the reserved pecan nuts over the top along with the demerara sugar and nutmeg.

6 Bake for about 40 minutes until risen and golden, then serve warm, with cream, if you like.

Nutritional information per portion: Energy 291kcal/1227kJ; Protein 10g; Carbohydrate 46g, of which sugars 24g; Fat 9g, of which saturates 3g; Cholesterol 48mg; Calcium 189mg; Fibre 2.3g; Sodium 240mg.

Bread and butter pudding

A family favourite in the UK, bread and butter pudding was traditionally made to use up leftovers. Today it appears on the menus of upmarket restaurants, though this is the original version.

SERVES 4–6

50g/2oz/4 tbsp soft butter

6 large slices of day-old
white bread

50g/2oz dried fruit, such as raisins,
sultanas (golden raisins) or chopped
dried apricots

40g/1½ oz/3 tbsp caster
(superfine) sugar

2 large (US extra large) eggs

600ml/1 pint/2½ cups full cream
(whole) milk

cream, to serve (optional)

1 Preheat the oven to 160°C/325°F/Gas 5. Lightly butter a 1.2 litre/2 pint/5 cup ovenproof dish.

2 Butter the slices of bread and cut them into small triangles or squares. Arrange half the bread pieces, buttered side up, in the prepared dish and sprinkle the dried fruit and half of the sugar over the top.

3 Lay the remaining bread slices, again buttered side up, evenly on top of the fruit. Sprinkle the remaining sugar evenly over the top.

4 Beat the eggs lightly together and stir in the milk.

5 Strain the egg mixture and pour it over the bread in the dish. Push the top slices of bread down into the liquid if necessary so that it is all submerged.

6 Leave the pudding to stand for 30 minutes to allow the bread to soak up all the liquid (this is an important step, so don't be tempted to skip it).

7 Put the dish into the hot oven and cook for about 45 minutes or until the custard is set and the top is crisp and golden brown. Serve the pudding immediately, with cream, if you like.

Nutritional information per portion: Energy 622kcal/2597kJ; Protein 10.5g; Carbohydrate 55.6g, of which sugars 37.8g; Fat 39g, of which saturates 23g; Cholesterol 186mg; Calcium 203mg; Fibre 1.6g; Sodium 350mg.

Queen of puddings

This delicate British dessert has a base made with custard and breadcrumbs flavoured with lemon. Once it is set, a layer of jam is added and covered with a light meringue topping.

SERVES 4

80g/3oz/1½ cups fresh breadcrumbs
60ml/4 tbsp caster (superfine) sugar,
   plus 5ml/1 tsp
grated rind of 1 lemon
600ml/1 pint/2½ cups milk
4 eggs
45ml/3 tbsp raspberry jam, warmed

COOK'S TIP

The traditional recipe stipulates that raspberry jam should be used, but you could ring the changes by replacing it with a different jam, such as strawberry or plum, or with lemon curd, marmalade or fruit purée.

1 Stir the breadcrumbs, 30ml/2 tbsp of the sugar and the lemon rind together in a bowl. Bring the milk to the boil in a pan. Stir it into the breadcrumb mixture.

2 Separate three of the eggs and beat the yolks with the remaining whole egg. Stir the eggs into the breadcrumb mixture, then pour into a buttered ovenproof dish and leave to stand for 30 minutes.

3 Meanwhile, preheat the oven to 160°C/325°F/Gas 3. Cook the pudding for 50–60 minutes, until set.

4 Whisk the egg whites in a large, clean bowl until stiff but not dry, then gradually whisk in the remaining 30ml/2 tbsp caster sugar until the mixture is thick and glossy, being careful not to overwhip the mixture.

5 Spread the jam over the set custard, then spoon over the meringue to cover the top. Sprinkle the remaining 5ml/1 tsp sugar over the meringue, then return to the oven for 15 minutes more, until the meringue is light golden. Serve warm.

Nutritional information per portion: Energy 297kcal/1259kJ; Protein 13.7g; Carbohydrate 45g, of which sugars 31g; Fat 8.5g, of which saturates 3.2g; Cholesterol 199mg; Calcium 242mg; Fibre 0.4g; Sodium 281mg.

Plum crumble

Fruit crumble is a perennially popular dessert. Plums can be divided into three categories –
dessert, dual and cooking. Choose whichever dual or cooking plum is available locally.

SERVES 4

450g/1lb stoned (pitted) plums
50g/2oz/¼ cup soft light brown sugar
15ml/1 tbsp water
juice of 1 lemon

FOR THE CRUMBLE TOPPING
50g/2oz/½ cup plain (all-purpose) flour
25g/1oz/generous ¼ cup coarse
   rolled oats
50g/2oz/¼ cup soft light brown sugar
50g/2oz/¼ cup butter, softened

1 Preheat the oven to 200°C/400°F/Gas 6. Place a large pan over a medium heat. Put the plums in the pan and add the sugar, water and lemon juice. Mix thoroughly and bring to the boil, stirring continuously until the sugar dissolves. Cook the plums until they are just beginning to soften. Place the fruit with the juices in a deep pie dish.

2 Place the crumble ingredients in a bowl and rub together with your fingers until the mixture resembles breadcrumbs.

3 Sprinkle the crumble topping evenly over the fruit, then bake the crumble in the preheated oven for 20 minutes, or until the top is crunchy and golden brown.

Nutritional information per portion: Energy 304kcal/1284kJ; Protein 2.9g; Carbohydrate 51.5g, of which sugars 37.4g; Fat 11.1g, of which saturates 6.5g; Cholesterol 27mg; Calcium 53mg; Fibre 2.8g; Sodium 82mg.

Apple and blackberry crumble

The origins of crumble are unclear. It did not appear in recipe books until the 20th century, but has become a firm favourite all over the UK. The oatmeal adds even more delicious crunch.

SERVES 6–8

115g/4oz/½ cup butter

115g/4oz/1 cup wholemeal
(whole-wheat) flour

50g/2oz/½ cup fine or medium oatmeal

50g/2oz/¼ cup soft light brown sugar

a little grated lemon rind (optional)

900g/2lb cooking apples

450g/1lb/4 cups blackberries

a squeeze of lemon juice

175g/6oz/scant 1 cup caster
(superfine) sugar

1 Preheat the oven to 200°C/400°F/Gas 6. To make the crumble, rub the butter into the flour, and then add the oatmeal and brown sugar and continue to rub in until the mixture begins to stick together, forming large crumbs.

2 Mix in the grated lemon rind if using. Peel and core the cooking apples and slice into wedges.

3 Put the apples, blackberries, lemon juice, 30ml/2 tbsp water and caster sugar in a shallow ovenproof dish, about 2 litres/3½ pints/9 cups capacity.

4 Cover the fruit with the crumble topping. Put into the hot oven and cook for 15 minutes, then reduce the heat to 190°C/375°F/Gas 5 and cook for 15–20 minutes until golden brown.

Nutritional information per portion: Energy 336kcal/1413kJ; Protein 4g; Carbohydrate 53.1g, of which sugars 30.8g; Fat 13.4g, of which saturates 6.8g; Cholesterol 27mg; Calcium 72mg; Fibre 3g; Sodium 81mg.

Hot blackberry and apple soufflés

The deliciously tart flavours of blackberry and apple complement each other perfectly to make a light, mouthwatering and surprisingly low-fat hot pudding.

SERVES 6

150g/5oz/³⁄₄ cup caster sugar,
   plus extra for dusting
350g/12oz/3 cups blackberries
1 large cooking apple, peeled and
   finely diced
grated rind and juice of 1 orange
3 egg whites
icing (confectioners') sugar, for dusting

COOK'S TIP

Running a table knife around the inside edge of the soufflé dishes before baking helps the soufflés to rise evenly without sticking to the rim of the dish.

1 Preheat the oven to 200°C/400°F/Gas 6. Generously grease six 150ml/ ¹⁄₄ pint/²⁄₃ cup individual soufflé dishes with butter and dust with caster sugar, shaking out the excess sugar. Put a baking sheet in the oven to heat.

2 Cook the blackberries, diced apple and orange rind and juice in a pan for 10 minutes or until the apple has pulped down. Press through a sieve (strainer) into a bowl. Stir in 50g/2oz/¹⁄₄ cup of the caster sugar. Set aside to cool.

3 Put a tablespoonful of the fruit purée into each prepared dish and smooth the surface. Set aside. Whisk the egg whites in a large grease-free bowl until they form stiff peaks. Very gradually whisk in the remaining caster sugar until glossy. Fold in the remaining fruit purée.

4 Spoon the mixture into the dishes. Level the tops with a palette knife or metal spatula, and run a table knife around the edge of each dish. Place on the hot baking sheet and bake for 10–15 minutes until the soufflés have risen and are lightly browned. Dust the tops with icing sugar and serve immediately.

Nutritional information per portion: Energy 123kcal/522kJ; Protein 2.1g; Carbohydrate 30.1g, of which sugars 30.1g; Fat 0.1g, of which saturates 0g; Cholesterol 0mg; Calcium 38mg; Fibre 2g; Sodium 33mg.

Hot chocolate soufflés

These rich, individual soufflés have the merest hint of orange flavour in them, and are divine served with the white chocolate sauce poured into the middle.

SERVES 6

45ml/3 tbsp caster (superfine) sugar,
 plus extra for dusting
175g/6oz plain (semisweet)
 chocolate, chopped
150g/5oz/²⁄₃ cup unsalted butter,
 cut in small pieces
4 large (US extra large) eggs, separated
30ml/2 tbsp orange liqueur (optional)

1.5ml/¹⁄₄ tsp cream of tartar
icing (confectioners') sugar, for dusting

FOR THE WHITE CHOCOLATE SAUCE

75g/3oz white chocolate, chopped
90ml/6 tbsp whipping cream
15–30ml/1–2 tbsp orange liqueur
grated rind of ¹⁄₂ orange

1 Generously grease six 150ml/¹⁄₄ pint/²⁄₃ cup ramekins. Sprinkle each with a little caster sugar and tap out any excess. Place the ramekins on a baking sheet. Melt the chocolate and butter in a bowl placed over a pan of simmering water, stirring constantly. Remove from the heat and cool slightly, then beat in the egg yolks and orange liqueur, if using. Set aside, stirring occasionally.

2 Preheat the oven to 220°C/425°F/Gas 7. In a large, grease-free bowl, whisk the egg whites slowly until frothy. Add the cream of tartar, increase the speed and whisk until the whites form soft peaks. Gradually sprinkle over the caster sugar, 15ml/1 tbsp at a time, whisking until the whites become stiff and glossy.

3 Stir a third of the whites into the cooled chocolate mixture to lighten it, then pour the mixture over the remaining whites. Using a rubber spatula or metal spoon, gently fold the sauce into the whites, cutting down to the bottom, then along the sides and up to the top in a semicircular motion until they are just combined; don't worry about a few white streaks. Spoon into the prepared dishes.

4 To make the white chocolate sauce, put the chopped white chocolate and the cream into a small pan. Place over a very low heat and warm, stirring constantly until melted and smooth. Remove from the heat and stir in the liqueur and orange rind, then pour into a jug (pitcher) and keep warm.

5 Bake the soufflés in the preheated oven for 10–12 minutes until risen and set, but still slightly wobbly in the centre. Dust with icing sugar and serve immediately with the warm white chocolate sauce.

Nutritional information per portion: Energy 239kcal/1010kJ; Protein 10.8g; Carbohydrate 39.9g, of which sugars 32.8g; Fat 5.8g, of which saturates 2.9g; Cholesterol 82mg; Calcium 97mg; Fibre 1.1g; Sodium 225mg.

Jam roly poly

This warming winter pudding, with its nursery-sounding name, first appeared on English tables in the 1800s and is now enjoyed throughout the world. Serve it thickly sliced with custard.

SERVES 4–6

175g/6oz/1½ cups self-raising (self-rising) flour

a pinch of salt

75g/3oz shredded suet (or vegetarian equivalent)

finely grated rind of 1 small lemon

90ml/6 tbsp jam

custard, to serve (optional)

COOK'S TIP

For the lightest suet pastry, use as little cold water as possible, and handle it as gently and lightly as you can.

1 Preheat the oven to 180°C/350°F/ Gas 4 and line a baking sheet with baking parchment.

2 Sift the flour and salt into a bowl and stir in the suet and lemon rind. With a round-ended knife, stir in just enough cold water to enable you to gather the mixture into a ball of soft dough, finishing off with your fingers.

3 Remove the ball of dough from the bowl, and on a lightly floured work surface or board, knead it very lightly until smooth. Roll it out into a 30 x 20cm/12 x 8in rectangle.

4 Using a palette knife or metal spatula, spread the jam evenly over the pastry, leaving all the edges clear. Brush the edges with a little water and, starting at one of the short ends, carefully roll up the pastry. Try to keep the roll fairly loose so that the jam is not squeezed out.

5 Place the roll, seam side down, on the prepared baking sheet. Bake it in the hot oven for 30–40 minutes until risen, golden brown and cooked through. Leave to cool for a few minutes before cutting into thick slices. Serve with custard, if you like.

Nutritional information per portion: Energy 240kcal/1008kJ; Protein 2.8g; Carbohydrate 33.7g, of which sugars 10.7g; Fat 11.3g, of which saturates 5.7g; Cholesterol 0mg; Calcium 104mg; Fibre 0.9g; Sodium 111mg.

Syrup sponge pudding

England is famous for its steamed puddings and this one is a classic. The light sponge with its golden coat of syrup brings back memories of childhood. Serve this one with custard or cream.

SERVES 4–6

45ml/3 tbsp golden (light corn) syrup

115g/4oz/8 tbsp soft butter, plus extra
   for greasing

115g/4oz/½ cup caster (superfine) sugar

2 eggs, beaten

5ml/1 tsp finely grated lemon rind

175g/6oz/1½ cups self-raising
   (self-rising) flour

30ml/2 tbsp milk

VARIATIONS

• *Replace the golden syrup with orange or lemon marmalade, or jam such as raspberry or plum.*

• *Add a few drops of vanilla extract in place of the lemon rind.*

1 Grease a 1.2 litre/2 pint/5 cup heatproof bowl and spoon the golden syrup into the bottom of it.

2 Beat the butter and sugar until pale, light and fluffy. Gradually beat in the eggs together with the lemon rind. Sift in the flour and fold it in using a metal spoon. Gently stir in the milk to give a soft dropping consistency. Spoon the mixture into the bowl.

3 Cover with a sheet of baking parchment, making a pleat in the centre to give it room to rise.

4 Cover this with a large sheet of foil, pleated in the centre. Tie string securely around the bowl, under the lip, to hold the foil and paper in place.

5 Half-fill a large pan with water and bring it to the boil. Place an inverted saucer in the bottom and stand the bowl on it. Cover the pan and steam the pudding for 1½ hours, adding more boiling water if necessary.

6 Allow the pudding to stand for 5 minutes before turning out on to a warm plate to serve.

Nutritional information per portion: Energy 480kcal/2005kJ; Protein 16.2g; Carbohydrate 48.2g, of which sugars 23.7g; Fat 27g, of which saturates 15.8g; Cholesterol 173mg; Calcium 153mg; Fibre 1.2g; Sodium 451mg.

Sticky toffee pudding

A truly indulgent classic, this dessert will always go down a treat. It's almost a meal in itself so make sure the main course is not too filling!

SERVES 6

115g/4oz/1 cup toasted walnuts, chopped
175g/6oz/¾ cup butter
175g/6oz/scant 1 cup soft dark
   brown sugar
60ml/4 tbsp double (heavy) cream
30ml/2 tbsp lemon juice
2 eggs, beaten
115g/4oz/1 cup self-raising
   (self-rising) flour

1 Grease a 900ml/1½ pint/¾ cup heatproof bowl and put in half the nuts.

2 Heat 50g/2oz/4 tbsp of the butter with 50g/2oz/4 tbsp of the sugar, the cream and 15ml/1 tbsp lemon juice in a small pan, stirring until smooth. Pour half into the heatproof bowl, then swirl to coat it a little way up the sides.

3 Beat the remaining butter and sugar until fluffy, then beat in the eggs. Fold in the flour, remaining nuts and lemon juice and spoon into the bowl.

4 Cover the bowl with baking parchment with a pleat folded in the centre, then tie securely with string. Place on an inverted saucer in a large pan half full of boiling water, and steam the pudding over a low heat for about 1¼ hours, until set in the centre.

5 Just before serving, gently warm the remaining sauce. Unmould the pudding on to a warm plate and pour over the warm sauce.

Nutritional information per portion: Energy 606kcal/2523kJ; Protein 7.5g; Carbohydrate 46g, of which sugars 31.6g; Fat 44.9g, of which saturates 20.3g; Cholesterol 152mg; Calcium 122mg; Fibre 1.3g; Sodium 279mg.

Sticky coffee and ginger pudding

This coffee-capped feather-light sponge is made with breadcrumbs and ground almonds.
Serve with creamy custard or scoops of vanilla ice cream for a grown-up nursery pudding.

SERVES 4

30ml/2 tbsp soft light brown sugar

25g/1oz/2 tbsp preserved stem ginger,
    chopped, plus 75ml/5 tbsp
    ginger syrup

30ml/2 tbsp mild-flavoured
    ground coffee

115g/4oz/generous ½ cup caster
    (superfine) sugar

3 eggs, separated

25g/1oz/¼ cup plain (all-purpose) flour

5ml/1 tsp ground ginger

65g/2½ oz/generous 1 cup fresh
    white breadcrumbs

25g/1oz/¼ cup ground almonds

1 Preheat the oven to 180°C/350°F/Gas 4. Grease and line the base of a 750ml/1¼ pint/3 cup ovenproof bowl with baking parchment. Sprinkle in the brown sugar and chopped ginger. Put the ground coffee in a small bowl.

2 Heat the ginger syrup until almost boiling, then pour into the coffee. Stir well and leave for 4 minutes. Pour through a strainer into the ovenproof bowl.

3 Beat half the caster sugar with the egg yolks until light and fluffy. Sift the flour and ground ginger together, then fold into the egg yolk mixture with the breadcrumbs and ground almonds. Whisk the whites until stiff, then gradually whisk in the remaining sugar. Fold into the mixture, in two batches.

4 Spoon into the ovenproof bowl and smooth the top. Cover with a piece of pleated baking parchment and secure with string. Bake for 40 minutes, or until the sponge is firm to the touch. Turn out and serve immediately.

Nutritional information per portion: Energy 382kcal/1617kJ; Protein 9.7g; Carbohydrate 70.6g, of which sugars 53.5g; Fat 8.9g, of which saturates 1.7g; Cholesterol 171mg; Calcium 93mg; Fibre 1g; Sodium 240mg.

Hot date puddings with toffee sauce

Fresh dates make this pudding less rich than a dried date version, but it is still a bit of an indulgence!
To peel the dates, squeeze them between your thumb and forefinger and the skins will pop off.

SERVES 6

50g/2oz/¼ cup butter, softened

75g/3oz/½ cup light muscovado
(brown) sugar

2 eggs, beaten

115g/4oz/1 cup self-raising (self-rising) flour

2.5ml/½ tsp bicarbonate of soda (baking soda)

175g/6oz/1 cup fresh dates, peeled,
stoned (pitted) and chopped

75ml/5 tbsp boiling water

10ml/2 tsp coffee and chicory essence

FOR THE TOFFEE SAUCE

75g/3oz/½ cup light muscovado (brown) sugar

50g/2oz/¼ cup butter

60ml/4 tbsp double (heavy) cream

30ml/2 tbsp brandy (optional)

1 Preheat the oven to 180°C/350°F/Gas 4. Place a baking sheet in the oven to heat up. Grease six individual pudding moulds. Cream the butter and sugar in a bowl until pale and fluffy. Gradually add the eggs, beating well after each addition.

2 Sift the flour and bicarbonate of soda together and fold into the creamed mixture. Put the dates in a heatproof bowl, pour over the boiling water and mash with a potato masher. Add the coffee and chicory essence, then stir the paste into the creamed mixture.

3 Spoon the mixture into the prepared moulds. Place on the hot baking sheet and bake for 20 minutes.

4 Meanwhile, make the toffee sauce. Put all the ingredients in a pan and heat very gently, stirring occasionally, until the mixture is smooth. Increase the heat and boil, stirring, for 1 minute.

5 Turn the warm puddings out on to individual dessert plates. Spoon a generous amount of sauce over each portion and serve immediately.

COOK'S TIP

The sauce is a great standby. Try it on poached apple or pear slices, over ice cream or with a steamed pudding.

Nutritional information per portion: Energy 892kcal/3726kJ; Protein 23g; Carbohydrate 73.7g, of which sugars 69.3g; Fat 58.4g, of which saturates 19g; Cholesterol 228mg; Calcium 226mg; Fibre 7.2g; Sodium 349mg.

Chocolate puddings with rum custard

With melting moments of chocolate in every mouthful, these puddings won't last long. The rum custard turns them into an adult dessert; for children, flavour the custard with vanilla instead.

SERVES 6

115g/4oz/¹/₂ cup butter
115g/4oz/¹/₂ cup soft light brown sugar
2 eggs, beaten
a few drops of vanilla extract
45ml/3 tbsp unsweetened cocoa powder, sifted
115g/4oz/1 cup self-raising (self-rising) flour
75g/3oz dark (bittersweet) chocolate, chopped
a little milk, warmed

FOR THE RUM CUSTARD

250ml/8fl oz/1 cup full cream (whole) milk
15ml/1 tbsp caster (superfine) sugar
2 egg yolks
10ml/2 tsp cornflour (cornstarch)
30–45ml/2–3 tbsp rum

1 Lightly grease six individual dariole moulds or a 1.2 litre/2 pint/5 cup heatproof bowl. Cream the butter and sugar until pale and creamy. Gently blend in the eggs and the vanilla extract.

2 Sift together the cocoa and flour, and fold gently into the egg mixture with the chopped chocolate and sufficient milk to give a soft dropping consistency.

3 Spoon the mixture into the moulds or bowl, cover with buttered baking parchment and tie down. Fill a pan with 2.5–5cm/1–2in water, place the pudding(s) in the pan, cover with a lid and bring to the boil. Steam the large pudding for 1¹/₂–2 hours and the individual puddings for 45–50 minutes, topping up with water if necessary. When firm, turn out on to warm plates.

4 To make the rum custard, bring the milk and sugar to the boil. Whisk together the egg yolks and cornflour, then pour on the hot milk, whisking constantly. Return the mixture to the pan and stir constantly while it slowly comes back to the boil. Allow the sauce to simmer gently as it thickens, stirring all the time. Remove from the heat and stir in the rum.

COOK'S TIP

To cook in the microwave, spoon into a 1.5 litre/2¹/₂ pint/6¹/₄ cup microwave-proof bowl. Cover loosely with clear film (plastic wrap) and microwave on full power for 5 minutes. Leave to stand for 5 minutes.

Nutritional information per portion: Energy 458kcal/1915kJ; Protein 8.3g; Carbohydrate 49g, of which sugars 31.5g; Fat 25.6g, of which saturates 14.5g; Cholesterol 186mg; Calcium 145mg; Fibre 1.8g; Sodium 302mg.

Steamed chocolate and fruit puddings

Some things always turn out well, including these wonderful little puddings. Dark, fluffy chocolate sponge with tangy cranberries and apple is served with a honeyed chocolate syrup.

SERVES 4

115g/4oz/²⁄₃ cup dark muscovado (molasses) sugar

1 eating apple

75g/3oz/³⁄₄ cup cranberries, thawed if frozen

115g/4oz/¹⁄₂ cup soft margarine

2 eggs

75g/3oz/²⁄₃ cup plain (all-purpose) flour

2.5ml/¹⁄₂ tsp baking powder

45ml/3 tbsp unsweetened cocoa powder

FOR THE CHOCOLATE SYRUP

115g/4oz plain (semisweet) chocolate, broken into squares

30ml/2 tbsp clear honey

15ml/1 tbsp unsalted butter

2.5ml/¹⁄₂ tsp vanilla extract

1 Prepare a steamer or half fill a pan with water and bring it to the boil. Grease four individual heatproof bowls. Sprinkle each bowl with a little muscovado sugar to coat well.

2 Peel and core the apple. Dice it into a bowl, add the cranberries and mix well. Divide equally among the prepared pudding bowls.

3 Place the remaining muscovado sugar in a mixing bowl. Add the margarine, eggs, flour, baking powder and cocoa; beat until combined and smooth.

4 Spoon the mixture into the heatproof bowls and tie a double layer of foil over each. Steam for about 45 minutes, topping up the boiling water as required, until the puddings are well risen and firm.

5 To make the syrup, mix the chocolate, honey, butter and vanilla extract in a small pan. Heat gently, stirring, until melted and smooth.

6 Run a knife around the edge of each pudding to loosen it, then turn out on to plates. Serve immediately, with the chocolate syrup.

Nutritional information per portion: Energy 672kcal/2811kJ; Protein 8.7g; Carbohydrate 73.1g, of which sugars 57.3g; Fat 40.4g, of which saturates 13.9g; Cholesterol 105mg; Calcium 84mg; Fibre 3.2g; Sodium 366mg.

Chocolate chip and banana pudding

Hot and steamy, this superb pudding is surprisingly light. It tastes extra special when served with a drizzle of hot chocolate sauce and a dollop of cold whipped cream.

SERVES 4

200g/7oz/1¾ cups self-raising (self-rising) flour

75g/3oz/6 tbsp unsalted butter

2 ripe bananas

75g/3oz/⅓ cup caster (superfine) sugar

60ml/4 tbsp milk

1 egg, beaten

60ml/4 tbsp plain (semisweet) chocolate chips or chopped chocolate

chocolate sauce and whipped cream, to serve

1 Prepare a steamer or half fill a pan with water and bring it to the boil. Grease a 1 litre/1¾ pint/4 cup heatproof bowl. Sift the flour into a bowl and rub in the butter until the mixture resembles breadcrumbs.

2 Mash the bananas in a bowl. Stir them into the flour and butter mixture, with the caster sugar.

3 Whisk the milk with the egg in a jug (pitcher) or bowl, then beat into the pudding mixture.

4 Stir in the chocolate chips or chopped chocolate.

5 Spoon the mixture into the prepared bowl, cover closely with a double layer of foil, tie with string, and steam for 2 hours, topping up the water as required.

6 Run a knife around the top of the pudding to loosen it, then turn it out on to a warm serving dish. Serve hot, with the chocolate sauce and a spoonful of whipped cream.

Nutritional information per portion: Energy 528kcal/2220kJ; Protein 8.1g; Carbohydrate 79.3g, of which sugars 40.9g; Fat 22g, of which saturates 13g; Cholesterol 89mg; Calcium 222mg; Fibre 2.5g; Sodium 320mg.

Christmas pudding

This pudding is eaten on Christmas Day in the UK, brought to the table doused in warm brandy or whisky and set alight. Serve with pouring cream and brandy butter (see page 217).

SERVES 12 (MAKES 2 PUDDINGS)

280g/10oz/5 cups fresh breadcrumbs

225g/8oz/1 cup light muscovado (brown) sugar

225g/8oz/1 cup currants

280g/10oz/2 cups raisins

225g/8oz/1⅓ cups sultanas (golden raisins)

50g/2oz/⅓ cup chopped mixed
   (candied) peel

115g/4oz/½ cup glacé (candied) cherries, halved

225g/8oz suet, shredded (or vegetarian equivalent)

2.5ml/½ tsp salt

10–20ml/2–4 tsp mixed (apple pie) spice

1 carrot, peeled and coarsely grated

1 apple, peeled, cored and finely chopped

grated rind and juice of 1 orange

2 large (US extra large) eggs, lightly whisked

450ml/¾ pint/scant 2 cups stout

1 Put the breadcrumbs, sugar, dried fruit, peel and cherries in a large mixing bowl. Add the suet, salt, mixed spice, carrot, apple and orange rind. Mix well.

2 Stir the orange juice, eggs and stout into the breadcrumbs. Leave overnight, stirring occasionally, if possible.

3 Butter two 1.2 litre/2 pint/5 cup heatproof bowls and put a circle of baking parchment in the bottoms. Stir the mixture and turn into the bowls.

4 Top with buttered circles of baking parchment, cover tightly with more layers of parchment and foil, and tie securely under the rim. Half-fill a pan with water, place the puddings in the pan, cover with a lid and bring to the boil. Steam for about 6–7 hours, topping up the pan with boiling water as necessary.

5 When the puddings are cooked through and set in the centre, remove them from the pan and allow to cool. Re-cover them with foil and store in a cool, dry place.

COOK'S TIP

When a pudding is required, steam it for another 2–3 hours and serve hot. Christmas puddings are made at least a month in advance (traditionally on 'stir-up Sunday' at the end of November).

Nutritional information per portion: Energy 448kcal/1902kJ; Protein 2.4g; Carbohydrate 99.8g, of which sugars 92.5g; Fat 7.1g, of which saturates 3.6g; Cholesterol 20mg; Calcium 67mg; Fibre 0.9g; Sodium 123mg.

Eve's pudding

The name "Mother Eve's pudding", from the biblical Eve, was first used in the 19th century for a boiled suet pudding filled with apples, from which this lighter sponge version developed.

SERVES 4–6

115g/4oz/½ cup butter

115g/4oz/½ cup caster (superfine) sugar

2 eggs, beaten

grated rind and juice of 1 lemon

90g/3¼ oz/scant 1 cup self-raising (self-rising) flour

40g/1½ oz/⅓ cup ground almonds

115g/4oz/½ cup soft light brown sugar

550–675g/1¼–1½ lb cooking apples, cored and thinly sliced

25g/1oz/¼ cup flaked (sliced) almonds

1 Preheat the oven to 180°C/350°F/Gas 4. Beat together the butter and caster sugar in a large mixing bowl until the mixture is very light and fluffy.

2 Gradually beat the eggs into the butter mixture, beating well after each addition, then fold in the lemon rind, flour and ground almonds.

3 Mix the brown sugar, apples and lemon juice and put the mixture into an greased ovenproof dish, spreading it out evenly.

4 Spoon the sponge mixture over the top in an even layer and right to the edges. Sprinkle the almonds over. Put into the hot oven and cook for 40–45 minutes until risen and golden brown.

Nutritional information per portion: Energy 507kcal/2128kJ; Protein 6.9g; Carbohydrate 65.5g, of which sugars 52.7g; Fat 26.1g, of which saturates 12g; Cholesterol 114mg; Calcium 91mg; Fibre 2.8g; Sodium 159mg.

Surprise lemon pudding

Although all the ingredients are mixed together, during cooking a tangy lemon sauce forms beneath a light topping, giving this lemon pudding a tasty surprise.

SERVES 4

75g/3oz/6 tbsp butter
175g/6oz/¾ cup soft light brown sugar
4 eggs, separated
grated rind and juice of 4 lemons
50g/2oz/½ cup self-raising
   (self-rising) flour
120ml/4fl oz/½ cup full cream
   (whole) milk
icing (confectioners') sugar, for dusting

VARIATION
This pudding is also delicious made with oranges instead of lemons.

1 Preheat the oven to 180°C/350°F/Gas 4. Grease an 18cm/7in soufflé dish and stand it in a roasting pan.

2 Beat the butter and sugar together in a large bowl until pale and very fluffy. Beat in one egg yolk at a time, beating well after each addition and gradually beating in the lemon rind and juice until well mixed; do not worry if the mixture curdles a little.

3 Sift the flour into the lemon mixture and stir until mixed, then gradually stir in the milk. Whisk the egg whites in a separate bowl until stiff, but not dry, then lightly, but thoroughly, fold into the lemon mixture in three batches.

4 Carefully pour the mixture into the soufflé dish, then pour boiling water into the roasting pan. Bake in the middle of the oven for 45 minutes, or until golden on top. Dust with icing sugar and serve immediately.

Nutritional information per portion: Energy 319kcal/1341kJ; Protein 7g; Carbohydrate 43.1g, of which sugars 33.8g; Fat 14.5g, of which saturates 8.1g; Cholesterol 126mg; Calcium 166mg; Fibre 0.4g; Sodium 190mg.

Honey pudding

The flavour of this Mediterranean pudding is characterized by molasses. It is particularly delicious served with a dollop of cool ricotta, which provides an appealing contrast.

SERVES 8

olive oil, for brushing

breadcrumbs, for sprinkling

8 eggs

300g/11oz/1½ cups sugar

50g/2oz/2½ tbsp black treacle (molasses)

50g/2oz/¼ cup clear honey

2.5ml/½ tsp ground cinnamon

5ml/1 tsp dried yeast

icing (confectioners') sugar, for dusting

ricotta or other soft white (farmer's)
    cheese, to serve (optional)

1 Preheat the oven to 180°C/350°F/Gas 4. Brush eight 4cm/1½ in square moulds with olive oil and sprinkle with breadcrumbs, shaking out the excess.

2 Beat the eggs in a bowl, then beat in all the remaining ingredients until well blended.

3 Divide the mixture among the prepared moulds and place them in a roasting pan. Add sufficient boiling water to come about halfway up the sides of the moulds and bake for about 15 minutes, until risen.

4 Give the puddings approximately 5 minutes to fully set and then serve still warm, dusted with icing sugar, with ricotta or other soft cheese, if you like.

Nutritional information per portion: Energy 267kcal/1133kJ; Protein 7g; Carbohydrate 50.7g, of which sugars 48.2g; Fat 5.7g, of which saturates 1.6g; Cholesterol 190mg; Calcium 88mg; Fibre 0.1g; Sodium 108mg.

Tapioca pudding

This is one of those desserts that provokes strong reactions. Most people either love it or loathe it, but it is very popular throughout Latin America, strewn with crunchy cashews.

SERVES 6

90g/3½ oz/generous ½ cup tapioca

750ml/1¼ pints/3 cups full-fat
   (whole) milk

1 cinnamon stick, bruised

45ml/3 tbsp caster (superfine) sugar

30ml/2 tbsp sliced fresh coconut and
   lime rind shavings or chopped cashew
   nuts, to decorate

VARIATION

*For coconut-flavoured tapioca pudding,
simply replace the milk with the same
quantity of coconut milk.*

1 Put the tapioca in a sieve (strainer) and rinse under cold running water. Drain and transfer to a heavy pan.

2 Pour in the milk and leave to soak for 30 minutes. Place the pan over a medium heat and bring to the boil. Add the bruised cinnamon stick, then lower the heat and simmer gently for 30 minutes, or until most of the milk has been absorbed. Stir occasionally to prevent the tapioca from sticking.

3 Stir in the sugar and simmer for 10 minutes. Remove the cinnamon stick and spoon the pudding into individual bowls. Sprinkle with fresh coconut and lime rind or, if using cashew nuts, lightly toast them in a dry frying pan and sprinkle over the puddings. Serve warm.

Nutritional information per portion: Energy 325kcal/1388kJ; Protein 1g; Carbohydrate 84.9g, of which sugars 57.4g; Fat 0.4g, of which saturates 0.2g; Cholesterol 0mg; Calcium 51mg; Fibre 1.8g; Sodium 74mg.

Lingonberry and semolina pudding

Semolina can be used to make a range of foods, including a number of desserts, as here.
Decorate the finished dish with a sprinkling of lingonberries for a truly stunning finale to a meal.

SERVES 4

1 litre/1¾ pints/4 cups water

300g/11oz lingonberries, bilberries or
   cranberries, plus extra to decorate

150g/5oz/scant 1 cup semolina

about 90g/3½ oz/½ cup caster
   (superfine) sugar

COOK'S TIP

*For added texture and flavour, you can
add extra fresh berries at the end of step 2.*

1 Put the water and berries in a pan and bring to the boil. Strain the liquid into a clean pan. Push the berries through a sieve (strainer) into the pan.

2 Put the semolina in the pan and, stirring constantly, return to the boil. Reduce the heat and simmer gently for 5 minutes, until the semolina is cooked. Add the sugar according to taste and the type of fruit used.

3 Turn the mixture into a bowl and, using an electric whisk, whisk for at least 5 minutes until light and frothy. Serve in individual serving dishes and sprinkle over a few berries to decorate.

Nutritional information per portion: Energy 246kcal/1050kJ; Protein 4.4g; Carbohydrate 59.3g, of which sugars 30.2g; Fat 0.8g, of which saturates 0g; Cholesterol 0mg; Calcium 22mg; Fibre 2g; Sodium 7mg.

Baked rice pudding

Rice pudding can be traced back to medieval England, when rice and sugar were expensive imports. Much later it became a nursery favourite, served with a dollop of jam.

SERVES 4

50g/2oz/4 tbsp butter, diced,
  plus extra for greasing
50g/2oz/¹⁄₄ cup pudding rice
30ml/2 tbsp soft light brown sugar
900ml/1¹⁄₂ pints/3³⁄₄ cups full cream
  (whole) milk
a small strip of lemon rind
freshly grated nutmeg
jam, to serve

1 Preheat the oven to 150°C/300°F/Gas 2. Butter a 1.2 litre/2 pint/5 cup shallow ovenproof dish.

2 Put the rice, sugar and butter into the dish and stir in the milk. Add the strip of lemon rind and sprinkle a little nutmeg over the surface. Put the pudding into the hot oven.

3 Cook the pudding for about 2 hours, stirring after 30 minutes and another couple of times during the next 1¹⁄₂ hours, until the rice is tender and the pudding is thick and creamy.

4 If you prefer skin on top, leave the pudding undisturbed for the final 30 minutes; if not, stir again. Serve with jam.

Nutritional information per portion: Energy 298kcal/1252kJ; Protein 8.8g; Carbohydrate 54.3g, of which sugars 21.5g; Fat 5.2g, of which saturates 1.4g; Cholesterol 143mg; Calcium 71mg; Fibre 0g; Sodium 185mg.

Prune rice pudding

This rice pudding is popular in Bulgaria and Romania, where each household has its own way of preparing it. It has a deep fruity flavour, which works well with the rich creaminess of the rice.

SERVES 6

10 large ready-to-eat prunes, stones removed, left whole or roughly chopped
30ml/2 tbsp plum brandy
200g/7oz/1 cup pudding rice

400ml/14fl oz/1⅔ cups double (heavy) cream
700ml/25fl oz/2¾ cups full cream (whole) milk
150g/5oz/¾ cup caster (superfine) sugar
75ml/5 tbsp orange flower water

1 Put the prunes in a shallow dish, cover with the plum brandy and leave them to soak for at least 1 hour. Preheat the oven to 180°C/350°F/Gas 4.

2 Combine the rice and two-thirds of the double cream in a heavy pan. Cook over a medium heat for 2–3 minutes. Stir, then add the milk and all but 30ml/2 tbsp of the caster sugar.

3 Cook the mixture over a low heat, stirring occasionally, for another 10–15 minutes, or until the rice grains are soft and the liquid has been almost totally absorbed by the rice.

4 Add the remaining double cream and the orange flower water, stir and set aside.

5 Divide the prunes and the soaking liquid among six small ovenproof dishes, then distribute the rice pudding on top.

6 Bake in the preheated oven for 8–10 minutes, or until the tops of the puddings are golden brown. Remove them from the oven and set aside to cool briefly. Serve while still warm.

Nutritional information per portion: Energy 640kcal/2668kJ; Protein 8.1g; Carbohydrate 68.6g, of which sugars 42g; Fat 40.6g, of which saturates 22.8g; Cholesterol 103mg; Calcium 196mg; Fibre 1.4g; Sodium 93mg.

Steamed coconut and mandarin custards with nut praline

These scented custards with a fabulous melt-in-the-mouth texture are best served warm. However, they are also delicious when chilled, making them perfect for hassle-free entertaining.

SERVES 4

200ml/7fl oz/scant 1 cup coconut cream
200ml/7fl oz/scant 1 cup double (heavy) cream
2.5ml/½ tsp finely ground star anise
75ml/5 tbsp golden caster (superfine) sugar
15ml/1 tbsp very finely grated mandarin or
   orange rind
4 egg yolks

FOR THE PRALINE

175g/6oz/scant 1 cup caster (superfine) sugar
50g/2oz/½ cup roughly chopped mixed nuts
   (cashews, almonds and peanuts)

1 Make the praline. Place the sugar in a non-stick wok with 15–30ml/1–2 tbsp water. Cook over a medium heat for 6–8 minutes, until the sugar dissolves and the mixture turns light gold.

2 Remove the syrup from the heat and pour on to a baking sheet lined with baking parchment. Spread out using the back of a spoon, then sprinkle the chopped nuts evenly over the top and leave to harden.

3 Meanwhile place the coconut cream, double cream, star anise, sugar, mandarin or orange rind and egg yolks in a large bowl. Whisk to combine and pour the mixture into four lightly greased ramekins or small, heatproof bowls.

4 Place the ramekins or bowls in a large steamer, cover and place in a wok and steam over gently simmering water for 12–15 minutes, or until the custards are just set.

5 Carefully lift the custards from the steamer and leave to cool slightly for about 10 minutes.

6 To serve, break up the praline into rough pieces and serve on top of, or alongside, the custards.

Nutritional information per portion: Energy 643kcal/2688kJ; Protein 6.7g; Carbohydrate 71g, of which sugars 69.3g; Fat 38.9g, of which saturates 19.6g; Cholesterol 270mg; Calcium 100mg; Fibre 0.4g; Sodium 115mg.

Tips, techniques and sauces for desserts

This chapter covers all the extra information you will need to make your dessert a success. It includes tips for mastering the art of pastry-making, including producing different types of pastry, lining tart tins and baking blind; essential techniques for preparing various kinds of fresh fruit, from passion fruit to pineapple; making classic ice creams and water ices; and finally, creating a medley of wonderful dessert sauces, which range from traditional Crème Anglaise to delectable Chocolate Fudge Sauce.

Making pastry

Good pastry is at the heart of many desserts, from crispy shortcrust tart bases to lighter-than-air choux profiteroles. The following pages provide all the know-how you will need, from making various types of pastry, to lining tins and tips for perfect baking.

SHORTCRUST PASTRY

A meltingly short, crumbly pastry is great for desserts as it sets off any filling to perfection. The fat content of the pastry dough can be made up of half butter or margarine and half white vegetable fat or with all one kind of fat. The ingredients here will make a 23cm/9in pastry case.

INGREDIENTS
225g/8oz/2 cups plain (all-purpose) flour
1.5ml/¼ tsp salt
115g/4oz/½ cup fat, diced

1 Sift the flour and salt into a bowl. Add the fat. Cut the fat with a pastry blender or rub it in with your fingertips until the mixture is crumb-like.

2 Sprinkle 45ml/3 tbsp of chilled water over the mixture. With a fork, toss gently to mix and moisten it.

3 Press the dough into a ball. If the dough is too dry to hold together, gradually add another 15ml/1 tbsp of chilled water.

4 Wrap the ball of dough with clear film (plastic wrap) or baking parchment and chill it for at least 30 minutes.

MAKING SHORTCRUST PASTRY IN A FOOD PROCESSOR

If you have hot hands, or the weather is warm, using a food processor ensures that the dough stays cool. It is wonderfully quick and easy.

1 Put the flour and salt in a food processor and process for 5 seconds.

2 Add the fat and process, turning the machine on and off, just until the mixture resembles fine breadcrumbs.

3 Add 45–60ml/3–4 tbsp of chilled water and process again briefly – just until the dough starts to pull away from the sides of the bowl. It should still look crumbly.

4 Gather the dough into a ball. Wrap it in clear film and chill for 30 minutes.

Shortcrust pastry variations

For Nut Shortcrust Add 30g/1oz/¼ cup finely chopped walnuts or pecan nuts to the flour mixture before adding the fat.

For Rich Shortcrust Use 225g/8oz/2 cups flour and 175g/6oz/¾ cup fat (preferably all butter), plus 15ml/1 tbsp caster (superfine) sugar, if you like. Bind the mixture with 1 egg yolk and 30–45ml/2–3 tbsp water.

For a Two-crust Pie Increase the proportions for these pastries by 50%, thus the amounts needed for basic shortcrust pastry are: 340g/12oz/3 cups flour, 2.5ml/½ tsp salt, 175g/6oz/¾ cup fat, 75–90ml/5–6 tbsp water.

FRENCH FLAN PASTRY

The pastry for tarts and flans is made with butter or margarine, giving a rich and crumbly result. The more fat used, the richer the pastry will be – almost like a biscuit dough – and the harder to roll out. If you have difficulty rolling it, you can press it into the flan tin (pan) instead, or roll it out between sheets of clear film (plastic wrap). Flan pastry, like shortcrust, can be made by hand or in a food processor. The ingredients here will make a 23cm/9in pastry case.

INGREDIENTS

200g/7oz/1³⁄₄ cups plain (all-purpose) flour
2.5ml/¹⁄₂ tsp salt
115g/4oz/¹⁄₂ cup butter or margarine
1 egg yolk
1.5ml/¹⁄₄ tsp lemon juice

1 Sift the flour and salt into a bowl. Add the butter or margarine. Rub into the flour until the mixture resembles fine breadcrumbs.

2 In a small bowl, mix the egg yolk, lemon juice and 30ml/2 tbsp of chilled water. Add to the flour mixture. With a fork, toss gently to mix and moisten.

3 Press the dough into a rough ball. If it is too dry to come together, add 15ml/1 tbsp more water. Turn the dough on to the work surface or a pastry board.

4 With the heel of your hand, knead the dough by pushing small portions of dough away from you, smearing them on the surface.

5 Continue mixing the dough in this way until it feels pliable and can be peeled easily off the work surface or pastry board.

6 Press the dough into a smooth ball. Wrap in clear film and chill it in the refrigerator for at least 30 minutes.

Flan pastry variations

For Sweet Flan Pastry Sift 200g/7oz/1³⁄₄ cups plain (all-purpose) flour with a pinch of salt and add 15g/¹⁄₂oz/1 tbsp caster (superfine) sugar. Rub or cut in 150g/5oz/10 tbsp butter and add 2 egg yolks mixed with 15–30ml/1–2 tbsp water and 2.5ml/¹⁄₂ tsp vanilla extract.

For Rich Flan Pastry This pastry has an extra egg yolk and more butter. It is ideal for lining larger flan and tranche tins (pans). Use 200g/7oz/1³⁄₄ cups plain (all-purpose) flour, 2.5ml/¹⁄₂ tsp salt, 150g/5oz/10 tbsp butter, diced, 2 egg yolks and 15–30ml/1–2 tbsp water.

For Rich Sweet Flan Pastry Make rich flan pastry, adding 45ml/3 tbsp caster sugar with the flour and, if you like, 2.5ml/¹⁄₂ tsp vanilla extract with the egg yolks.

Light Nut Crust Chopped toasted almonds or hazelnuts are excellent added to the pastry for fruit pies. Stir 40g/1¹⁄₂oz/¹⁄₃ cup finely chopped nuts into the flour mixture before adding any liquid.

CHOUX PASTRY

Unlike other pastries, with choux pastry the butter is melted with water and then the flour is added, followed by eggs. The result is more of a paste than a pastry. It is easy to make, but care must be taken in measuring the ingredients.

MAKES 18 PROFITEROLES OR 12 ÉCLAIRS

115g/4oz/½ cup butter, cut into small pieces
10ml/2 tsp caster (superfine) sugar (optional)
1.5ml/¼ tsp salt
150g/5oz/1¼ cups plain (all-purpose) flour
4 eggs, beaten to mix
1 egg, beaten with 5ml/1 tsp cold water, for glazing

1 Preheat the oven to 220°C/425°F/Gas 7. Combine the butter, sugar (if using), salt and 250ml/8fl oz/1 cup of water in a large, heavy pan. Bring to the boil over a medium-high heat, stirring occasionally.

2 As soon as the mixture boils, remove from the heat. Add the flour all in one go. Beat vigorously with a wooden spoon to blend the flour and liquid.

3 Return the pan to medium heat and cook, stirring, until the mixture will form a ball, pulling away from the side of the pan. This will take about 1 minute. Remove from the heat again and allow to cool for 3–5 minutes.

4 Add a little of the beaten eggs and beat well to incorporate. Add a little more egg and beat in well. Continue beating in the eggs until the mixture becomes a smooth and shiny paste.

5 While warm, spoon on to a baking sheet lined with baking parchment.

6 Glaze with 1 egg beaten with 1 teaspoon of cold water. Put into the preheated oven, then reduce the heat to 200°C/400°F/Gas 6. Bake until puffed and golden brown. Large puffs and éclairs will need 30–35 minutes, profiteroles will need 20–25 minutes, and rings will need 40–45 minutes.

Shaping choux pastry

For Large Puffs Use two large spoons dipped in water. Drop the paste in 5–6cm/2–2½in wide blobs on the paper-lined baking sheet, leaving 4cm/1½in between each. Neaten the blobs as much as possible. Alternatively, for well-shaped puffs, pipe the paste using a piping (pastry) bag fitted with a 2cm/¾in plain nozzle.

For Profiteroles Use two small spoons or a piping bag fitted with a 1cm/½in nozzle and shape 2.5cm/1in blobs.

For Éclairs Use a piping bag fitted with a 2cm/¾in nozzle. Pipe strips 10–13cm/4–5in long.

For a Ring Draw a 30cm/12in circle on the paper. Spoon the paste in large blobs on the circle to make a ring. Or pipe two rings around the circle and a third on top.

MAKING TARTS AND PIES

Once your pastry is prepared, you are ready to roll it and use it to make tasty tarts and luxurious pies, which can be filled with a whole host of sweet treats.

Rolling out pastry

To achieve a neat pastry case that doesn't distort or shrink in baking, handle the dough gently and avoid pulling or stretching it.

1 Remove the chilled dough from the refrigerator and allow it to soften slightly at room temperature. Unwrap it and put it on a lightly floured surface. Flatten the dough into a neat, round disc. Lightly flour the rolling pin.

2 Using even pressure, start rolling out the dough, working away from you from the centre to the far edge (but not over the edge) each time and easing the pressure slightly as you reach the edge.

3 Lift up the dough and give it a quarter turn from time to time during the rolling. This will prevent the dough sticking to the surface, and will help keep the thickness even.

4 Continue rolling out until the dough circle is about 5cm/2in larger all round than the tin (pan). It should be about 3mm/⅛in thick.

Lining a flan tin

1 Set the rolling pin on the dough, near one side of the circle. Fold the outside edge of the dough over the pin, then roll the pin over the dough to wrap the dough round it. Do this gently and loosely.

2 Hold the pin over the tin and gently unroll the dough so it drapes into the tin, centring it as much as possible.

3 With your fingertips, lift and ease the dough into the tin, gently pressing it over the bottom and up the side. Turn excess dough over the rim and trim it by rolling the rolling pin over it, or with a knife or scissors, depending on the edge to be made.

4 Prick the base all over with a fork to stop it rising during baking. Cover the pastry case with clear film (plastic wrap) and chill in the refrigerator for 30 minutes before baking.

Making a single-crust pie

This is when a single sheet of pastry covers a pie, and the filling goes directly into the pie dish.

1 Roll out the dough on a work surface until it is 3mm/⅛in thick and 5cm/2in larger all round than the dish.

2 Cut a 2cm/¾in strip from around the edge of the dough. Brush the rim of the dish with water and place the strip around the rim, pressing it down. Brush with water, then add the filling in a dome.

3 Using a rolling pin, place the dough over the filling. Seal the edges, trim off the excess and finish the edge. Glaze and make steam holes.

Quantity guide for flans and tarts
These pastry weights are a guide only, and refer to shortcrust pastry and its variations only. Figures given are the combined weight of ingredients.

Tin (pan) size	Pastry weight
18cm/7in	200g/7oz
20cm/8in	275g/10oz
23cm/9in	350g/12oz
25cm/10in	400g/14oz
4 x 10cm/4in	250g/9oz
6 x 7.5cm/3in	250g/9oz

Making a double-crust pie

A double-crust pie has the filling enclosed between two layers of pastry.

1 Roll out half the dough on a floured surface to 3mm/¹⁄₈in thick, and 5cm/ 2in larger all round than the dish. Wrap the rest in clear film (plastic wrap).

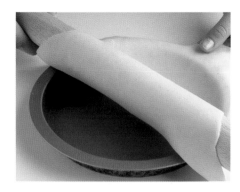

2 Wrap the dough loosely around the rolling pin. Holding the rolling pin over the pie dish, gently unroll the dough away from you so that it drapes into the dish, centring it as much as possible.

3 With floured fingers, press the dough over the base and up the sides, without stretching it. Trim off the excess.

4 Spoon the filling into the dish in a dome. Brush the edge of the dough with water. Roll out the remaining dough to a round larger than the top of the pie. Roll it up around the rolling pin and unroll over the pie. Press the edges together.

5 Hold the pie dish in one hand and cut off the excess dough with a knife, holding the blade at a slight angle. Reserve the trimmings for decorations. Glaze and make steam holes.

FINISHING THE EDGE

There are many options for making pretty decorative edges for your sweet pies and tarts.

Forked edge

Trim the dough even with the rim and press it flat. Firmly and evenly press the prongs of a fork all round the edge. If the fork sticks, dip it in flour every so often.

Crimped edge

Trim the dough to leave an overhang of about 1.5cm/¹⁄₂in all round. Fold the extra dough under. Put the knuckle or tip of the index finger of one of your hands inside the edge, pointing directly out. With the thumb and index finger of your other hand, pinch the dough edge around your index finger into a 'V' shape. Continue all the way round the edge.

Cutout edge

Trim the dough even with the rim and press it flat on the rim. With a small pastry cutter, cut out decorative shapes from the dough trimmings. Moisten the edge of the pastry case and press the cutouts in place, overlapping them slightly if you like.

Ruffled edge

Trim the dough to leave an overhang of about 1.5cm/¹⁄₂in all round the edge. Fold the extra dough under. Hold the thumb and index finger of one of your hands about 2.5cm/1in apart, inside the edge, pointing directly out. With the index finger of your other hand, gently pull the dough between them, to the end of the rim. Continue this all the way round the edge.

Ribbon edge

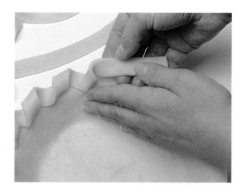

Trim the dough even with the rim and press it flat. Cut long strips about 2cm/³⁄₄in wide from the dough trimmings. Moisten the edge and press one end of a strip on to it. Twist the strip gently and press it on to the edge again. Continue all the way round the edge.

BAKING TARTS AND PIES

When you are ready to bake your tart or pie, there are a few simple rules that will ensure perfect results. Always preheat the oven for about 15 minutes to reach the required temperature. In conventional (not fan-assisted) ovens bake pastry on the middle shelf or just above the middle of the oven, unless otherwise stated. When blind-baking or cooking a double-crust pie, heat a heavy baking sheet in the oven. The hot sheet will help make the bottom of the pastry crisp.

Baking times may vary depending on your oven and how chilled the pie was. Check the pie at least 5 minutes before the end of the suggested cooking time. Don't keep opening the oven door though, or heat will be lost, and the pastry will be less crisp.

Baking shortcrust pastry

Shortcrust pastry and its variations should be well chilled before baking to minimize shrinkage. Between 30 and 60 minutes is adequate for a flan or pie that is filled prior to baking. If a flan case is to be blind-baked or filled just before baking, chill for an hour uncovered, or cover with clear film (plastic wrap) and chill overnight.

Shortcrust-type pastries are usually baked at 200°C/400°F/Gas 6, but often the temperature is reduced part-way through baking to allow the filling to cook sufficiently. Sweet pastries that contain sugar need to be removed from the oven as soon as the pastry is golden brown, or they can burn very quickly.

Don't cook foods that release a lot of steam at the same time as the shortcrust is cooking. This could stop the pastry from becoming crisp.

Baking blind

This process is used to partly cook an empty pastry case so that it does not become soggy when the filling is added. It is also used to completely bake a case when the filling cooks in a short time and you need to ensure that the pastry is fully cooked, and when the case is to contain a filling that does not require any cooking, such as Boston Banoffee Pie.

Lining the pastry case with baking parchment or foil and filling it with baking beans stops the pastry from rising up during cooking.

1 Cut out a round of baking parchment or foil about 7.5cm/3in larger than the tin. Prick the base of the case all over with a fork.

2 Press the baking parchment or foil smoothly over the base of the case and up the sides.

3 Evenly spread commercially made ceramic baking beans, or dried beans, over the base of the case.

4 To partially bake, place in a preheated oven at 200°C/400°F/Gas 6 for 15 minutes until the pastry is set and the rim is dry and golden. Lift out the paper and beans. Bake for a further 5 minutes. The pastry case can now be filled and the baking completed.

5 For fully baked pastry, bake at 200°C/400°F/Gas 6 for 15 minutes, then remove the paper and beans and return to the oven. Bake for a further 5–10 minutes, or until golden brown. Cool completely before filling.

6 Allow 6–8 minutes for partial baking of tartlets, and 12–15 minutes for fully baked pastry.

Baking tips for success
• Repair any holes in the cooked pastry by brushing with beaten egg, then return to the oven for 2–3 minutes to seal. For larger holes, press a little raw pastry into the gap, brush with egg, then return to the oven.
• If the pastry starts to bubble up during baking, remove it from the oven, prick again with a fork to release the air and return to the oven. If it has bubbled up at the end of baking, make a small slit in the bubble with a knife.

Preparing fresh fruit

Fruit is great to use in a vast range of desserts as it provides natural sweetness and a range of textures. People are often afraid to use unfamiliar or exotic fruits, but this section explains how to prepare them.

PEELING AND TRIMMING FRESH FRUIT

Most fruits will require peeling before being used in desserts.

Citrus fruits

To peel completely: cut a slice from the top and from the base. Set the fruit base down on a work surface. Using a small sharp knife, cut off the peel lengthways in thick strips. Take the coloured rind and all the white pith (which has a bitter taste). Cut, following the curve of the fruit.
To remove rind use a vegetable peeler to cutoff the rind in wide strips, taking none of the white pith. Use these strips whole or cut them into fine shreds with a sharp knife, according to recipe directions. Or rub the fruit against the fine holes of a metal grater, turning the fruit so you take just the coloured rind and not the white pith. Or use a special tool, called a citrus zester, to take fine threads of rind. (Finely chop the threads as an alternative method to grating.)

Kiwi fruit

Follow the citrus fruit technique, taking off the peel in thin lengthways strips.

Apples, pears, quinces, mangoes, papayas

Use a small sharp knife or a vegetable peeler. Take off the peel in long strips, as thinly as possible.

Peaches, apricots

Cut a cross in the base using a small sharp knife. Immerse the fruit in boiling water. Leave for 10–30 seconds (according to ripeness), then drain and immerse in iced water. The skin should slip off easily.

Pineapples

First cut off the leafy crown, then cut a slice from the base and set the pineapple upright. With a sharp knife, cut off the peel lengthways, cutting thickly to remove the brown 'eyes' with the peel.

Bananas, lychees, avocados

Make a small cut in the skin, then you should be able to remove it easily with your fingers.

Passion fruit, pomegranates

Cut in half horizontally, or cut a slice off the top of the fruit. With a spoon, scoop the flesh and seeds into a bowl.

Star fruit (carambola)

Trim off the tough, darkened edges of the five segments.

Rhubarb

Cut off and discard the leaves (they are poisonous). Peel off any tough skin.

Fresh currants

Pull each cluster through the prongs of a fork to remove the currants from the stalks.

Fresh dates

Squeeze gently at the stalk end to remove the rather tough skin.

CORING AND STONING (PITTING) OR SEEDING FRUIT

Whether a fruit has large stones (pits) or tiny seeds, it is often best to remove them.

Apples, pears, quinces

For whole fruit: use an apple corer to stamp out the whole core from stalk end to base. Alternatively, working up from the base, use a melon baller to cut out the core, leaving the stalk end intact.
For halves: use a melon baller to scoop out the core. Cut out the stalk and base using a small sharp knife.
For quarters: cut out the stalk and core with a serrated knife.

Citrus fruit

With the tip of a pointed knife, nick out pips (seeds) from slices or segments.

Cherries

Use a cherry stoner (pitter) to achieve the neatest results.

Peaches, apricots, nectarines, plums

Cut the fruit in half, cutting round the indentation and not along it. Twist the halves apart. Lift out the stone, or lever it out with the tip of a sharp knife.

Fresh dates

Cut the fruit lengthways in half and lift out the stone. Or, if the fruit is to be used whole, cut in from the stalk end with a thin-bladed knife to loosen the stone, then remove it.

Mangoes

Cut lengthways on either side of the large flat stone in the centre. Curve the cut slightly to follow the shape of the stone. Cut the flesh from the two thin ends of the stone.

Papayas, melons

Cut the fruit in half. Scoop out the seeds from the central hollow, then scrape away any fibres.

Pineapples

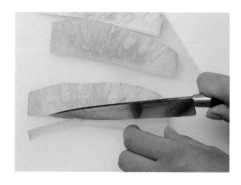

For spears and wedges: cut out the core neatly with a sharp knife.
For rings: cut out the core with a small pastry (cookie) cutter.

Gooseberries

Use scissors to trim off the stalk and flower ends.

Grapes

Cut the fruit lengthways in half. Use a small knife to nick out the pips. Or use the curved end of a sterilized hair grip.

Star fruit (carambola), watermelons

Use the tip of a knife to nick out pips.

Strawberries

Use a special huller to remove leafy green top and central core. Or cut these out with a small sharp knife.

Avocados

Cut the fruit in half lengthways. Stick the tip of a sharp knife into the stone and lever it out without damaging the surrounding flesh.

CUTTING FRUIT

How you cut the fruit will depend on the recipe you are making.

Apples, quinces

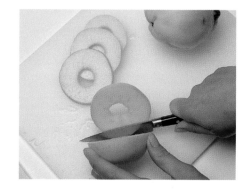

For rings: remove the core and seeds with an apple corer. Set the fruit on its side and cut across into rings.
For slices: cut the fruit in half and remove core and seeds with a melon baller. Set one half cut side down and cut it across into neat slices. Or cut the fruit into quarters and remove core and seeds with a knife. Cut lengthways into neat slices.

Pears

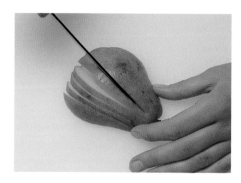

For fans: cut the fruit in half and remove the core and seeds with a melon baller. Set one half cut side down and cut lengthways into thin slices, not cutting all the way through at the stalk end. Gently fan out the slices so they are overlapping evenly. Carefully transfer the pear fan to a plate or pastry case using a palette knife or metal spatula.

For slices: follow apple technique.

Citrus fruit

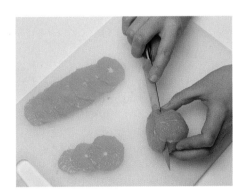

For slices: using a serrated knife, cut the peeled fruit crossways into neat even slices.

For segments: hold the peeled fruit in your cupped palm, over a bowl to catch the juice. Working from the side of the fruit to the centre, slide the knife down one side of a separating membrane to free the flesh from it.

Then slide the knife down the other side of that segment to free it from the membrane there. Drop the segment into the bowl. Continue cutting out the segments, folding back the membrane like the pages of a book as you work. When all the segments have been cut out, squeeze the juice from the membrane.

Peaches, nectarines, apricots, plums

For slices: follow apple technique.

Papayas, avocados

For slices: follow apple technique. Or cut the unpeeled fruit into wedges, removing the central seeds or stone. Set each wedge peel side down and slide the knife down the length to cut the flesh away from the peel.

For fans: follow pear technique.

Melons

For slices: follow papaya technique.

For balls: use a melon baller.

Pineapples

For spears: cut the peeled fruit lengthways in half and then into quarters. Cut each quarter into spears and cut out the core.

For chunks: cut the peeled fruit into spears. Remove the core. Cut across each spear into chunks.

For rings: cut the peeled fruit across into slices. Stamp out the central core from each slice using a pastry (cookie) cutter.

Kiwi fruit, star fruit (carambola)

Cut the fruit across into neat slices; discard the ends.

Mangoes

Cut the peeled mango flesh into either slices or cubes, according to the recipe directions.

Bananas

Cut the fruit across into neat even slices. Or cut the banana in half and then cut each half lengthways so you have four quarters.

Making ice cream

Many classic ice creams are based on a simple custard made from eggs and milk. It is not difficult to make, but as it is used so frequently, it is worth perfecting by following these very simple guidelines.

MAKING THE CUSTARD BASE
flavouring to infuse (optional)
300ml/½ pint/1¼ cups semi-skimmed (low-fat) milk
4 egg yolks
75g/3oz/6 tbsp caster (superfine) sugar
5ml/1 tsp cornflour (cornstarch)

1 By hand Prepare any flavourings. Split vanilla pods (beans) with a sharp knife; crack coffee beans with a mallet. You can use cinnamon sticks, whole cloves, fresh rosemary, lavender sprigs and bay leaves as they are.

2 Pour the milk into a pan. Bring it to the boil, then remove the pan from the heat, add the chosen flavouring and leave to infuse for 30 minutes or until cool. Remove the flavouring.

3 If you have used a vanilla pod, scrape the seeds back into the milk to enrich the flavour, using a small, sharp knife.

4 Whisk the egg yolks, caster sugar and cornflour in a bowl until thick and foamy. Bring the plain or infused milk to the boil, then gradually whisk it into the yolk mixture. Pour the combined mixture back into the pan.

5 Cook the custard mixture over a low heat, stirring constantly until it approaches boiling point and thickens to the point where the custard will coat the back of a wooden spoon. Do not let it overheat or it may curdle. Then take the pan off the heat and continue stirring, making sure that you take the spoon right around the bottom edges of the pan, until it has cooled slightly.

6 Pour the custard into a bowl and cover the surface with clear film (plastic wrap) to prevent the formation of a skin, or cover the surface with a light sprinkling of caster sugar. Leave to cool, then chill until required.

7 Using an ice cream maker: Follow steps 1–5 as above but ensure the custard is chilled before starting.

Rescuing curdled custard
Quickly take the pan off the heat and plunge it into a sink half filled with cold water. Stir frequently, taking the spoon right into the bottom edges of the pan. Keep stirring for 4–5 minutes until the temperature of the custard has dropped and the custard has stabilized. You may also find it helpful to whisk the mixture. If all else fails, sieve (strain) it.

USING FLAVOURINGS

1 By hand: If you haven't infused the milk, you may wish to flavour the custard. To make chocolate custard, stir pieces of white, dark (bittersweet) or milk chocolate into the hot custard in the pan, off the heat. Stir occasionally for 5 minutes until the chocolate has melted completely. Pour the flavoured custard into a bowl, and then cover and cool. Chill in the refrigerator.

2 Add other flavourings such as strong coffee (either filter or instant dissolved in boiling water), flower waters such as orange flower or rose water, or use sweeteners that also add flavour, such as maple syrup or honey. Vanilla, peppermint and almond extract are popular flavourings. You should add these to the custard after it has cooled.

ADDING CREAM

1 Using an ice cream maker: If you are making ice cream in an ice cream maker, make sure that you always follow the preliminary instructions for your specific machine, pre-cooling the machine or chilling the bowl in the freezer. Stir whipping cream, whipped double (heavy) cream or any soft cream cheeses into the chilled plain or flavoured custard and then churn until firm.

2 Creams with a high fat proportion – double cream, clotted cream or crème fraîche – should only be added to ice creams that are partially frozen, as they have a tendency to become buttery if churned for too long. Double cream can sometimes be added at the start of the process, but only for small quantities and minimal churning times.

By hand: Make the ice cream by hand in a freezerproof container by folding soft whipped cream into the chilled plain or flavoured custard and pouring into the tub. Allow enough space for beating the ice cream during freezing. Crème fraîche, clotted cream and cream cheeses can also be added at this stage.

Fruit and cream combinations
The combination of custard, cream and fruit purée can sometimes be too rich and just dulls the fruit flavour. So you can just use sieved (strained) fresh berry fruit purées, or poached and puréed orchard fruits stirred into whipped cream. If using an ice cream maker, partially freezing the purée before stirring in the cream speeds up the churning time.

MAKING A BASIC PARFAIT

Made correctly, a parfait is a light, cream-based confection with a softer, smoother texture than ice cream. It does not need beating during freezing, so is easy to make without an electric ice cream maker.

Parfaits can be set in moulds, tall glasses, china dishes or chocolate cups. The secret lies in the sugar syrup. Dissolve the sugar gently without stirring so that it does not crystallize, then boil rapidly until it registers 119°C/238°F on a sugar thermometer. This is the soft ball stage.

Quickly whisk the syrup into the whisked eggs. Cook over hot water until very thick. Cool, then mix with flavourings, alcohol and whipped cream. Freeze until solid and serve straight from the freezer.

Other flavourings

Usually made with coffee, parfaits are also delicious made with spices and fruit, such as cinnamon with apple or ginger with banana. Double (heavy) cream adds richness, and crème fraîche and whipping cream are good too. Or, for something more sophisticated, try fruit purées mixed with Kirsch, Cointreau or Grand Marnier.

SERVES FOUR

115g/4oz/generous ½ cup caster (superfine) sugar
120ml/4fl oz/½ cup water
4 egg yolks
flavourings
300ml/½ pint/1¼ cups double (heavy) cream

1 Gently heat the sugar and water in a pan, without stirring, until the sugar dissolves. Half fill a medium pan with water and bring to simmering point.

2 Bring the sugar syrup to the boil and boil rapidly for 4–5 minutes until it starts to thicken. It will be ready to use when it registers 119°C/238°F on a sugar thermometer, or forms a soft ball when dropped into water.

3 Whisk the egg yolks in a heatproof bowl until frothy. Place over the simmering water and gradually whisk in the hot sugar syrup. Whisk steadily until creamy. Take off the heat. Whisk until cool and the whisk leaves a trail across the surface when lifted.

4 Fold in the chosen flavourings, such as melted chocolate and brandy, ground cinnamon and coffee, whisky

and chopped ginger, Kirsch and raspberry purée, or kir and strawberry purée. In a separate bowl, whip the cream lightly until it just holds its shape. Fold it into the mixture.

5 Pour the parfait mixture into moulds, dishes or chocolate-lined cases. Freeze for at least 4 hours or until firm. Decorate, if you like, with whipped cream, spoonfuls of crème fraîche, chocolate-dipped fruits or caramel shapes. Serve immediately.

BOILING SUGAR

1 If you don't have a thermometer, check whether the sugar syrup is at the soft ball stage by lowering a spoon into it and lifting it up. If the syrup falls steadily from the spoon, it is not ready. Cook for a little longer.

2 The syrup is ready to test when it looks tacky and forms pliable strands when two spoons are dipped in it, back to back, and then pulled apart.

Take the pan off the heat and test by dropping a little boiling syrup into a bowl of iced water. It should form a solidified ball. Wait a few seconds until it cools, then lift it out. You should be able to mould it with your fingertips.

3 Once the syrup has reached soft ball stage, prevent it overcooking by plunging the base of the pan into cold water – either in a sink or in a shallow container. If the syrup is allowed to overcook, it will crystallize in the pan, forming brittle, glass-like strands, which snap. Adding over-cooked syrup to the eggs will cause the mixture to solidify into a rock-solid mass that is impossible to mix.

FREEZING ICE CREAM

Freezing is a crucial stage in the making of home-made ice cream and there are two basic freezing methods: 'still freezing' (freezing without a machine); and 'stir freezing' (using an ice cream maker). Making ice cream by hand requires freezing it in a tub or similar container and beating it several times during the freezing process. This process is all done automatically in an ice cream maker.

The secret of a really good ice cream is minute ice crystals. The finished ice cream should be light and cold but not icy. If the crystals are large, the ice cream will have a grainy, coarse texture, which will detract from the taste. Beating the ice cream, either by hand or with an ice cream maker, breaks down the crystals. The more it is beaten while it is freezing, the finer and silkier the finished texture.

FREEZING WITH AN ICE CREAM MAKER

1 Prepare your ice cream maker according to the manufacturer's instructions. Then pour the chilled custard and whipping cream into the bowl, fit the paddle, fix on the lid and begin churning.

2 After 10–15 minutes of churning, the ice cream will have begun to freeze. The mixture will thicken and will start to look slushy. Continue to churn in the same way.

3 After 20–25 minutes of churning, the ice cream will be considerably thicker but still too soft to scoop. This is the ideal time to mix in any of your chosen additional flavourings such as praline, liqueurs, purées or browned breadcrumbs.

ABOVE: *Electric machines take a lot of the hard work out of making ice cream.*

Making water ices

Water ices – sorbets and granitas – are made with a light sugar syrup flavoured with fruit juice, fruit purée, wine, liqueur, tea or herbs. They do not contain milk or cream, and are best made in an ice cream maker, as the constant churning ensures that the ice crystals are very tiny, for a smooth texture.

MAKING A BASIC SORBET

SERVES 6

150–200g/5–7oz/³/₄–1 cup caster (superfine) sugar

200–300ml/7–10fl oz/ ³/₄–1¹/₄ cups water

flavouring

1 egg white

1 Put the sugar and water in a medium pan and heat the mixture, stirring, until the sugar just dissolves.

2 Add pared citrus rinds, herbs or spices, depending on your chosen flavouring. Leave to infuse. Strain and cool, then chill well.

3 Mix with additional flavourings such as fruit juices, sieved (strained) puréed fruits, herbs or tea.

4 Using an ice cream maker: Pour the syrup mixture into the machine and churn until it is thick but still too soft to scoop.

5 Lightly beat the egg white with a fork and pour it into the ice cream maker, either through the top vent or by removing the lid completely, depending on the make. Continue churning until the sorbet is firm enough to scoop with a spoon.

Making fruit purées

As an approximate guide, 500g/ 1¹/₄ lb/5 cups of berry fruits will produce about 450ml/³/₄ pint/ scant 2 cups purée. Mix this with 115g–150g/4–5oz/generous

6 By hand: Pour the mixture into a plastic tub or similar freezerproof container. It should not be more than 4cm/1¹/₂in deep. Cover and freeze in the coldest part of the freezer for 4 hours or until it has partially frozen and ice crystals have begun to form. Beat until smooth with a fork, or hand-held electric whisk. Alternatively, process in a food processor until smooth.

7 Lightly beat the egg white and stir it into the sorbet. Freeze until firm enough to scoop (about 4 hours).

¹/₂–³/₄ cup caster (superfine) sugar (depending on natural acidity), dissolved in 300ml/¹/₂ pint/1¹/₄ cups boiling water and made up to 1 litre/1³/₄ pints/4 cups with extra cold water, lemon or lime juice.

MAKING GRANITAS
Citrus granita

This wonderfully refreshing, simple Italian-style water ice has the fine texture of snow and is most often served piled into pretty glass dishes. You don't need fancy or expensive equipment, just a medium pan, a sieve (strainer) or blender for puréeing the fruit, a fork and room in the freezer for a large plastic container.

Ingredients

There are no hard-and-fast rules when it comes to the proportions of sugar to water, nor is there a standard amount of flavouring which must be added. Unlike sorbets, granitas consist largely of water, with just enough sugar to sweeten them and prevent them from freezing too hard.
A total of 1 litre/1¾ pints/4 cups of flavoured sugar syrup will provide six generous portions of granita.

1 Juice and grate the rind of six lemons or oranges, or four ruby (pink) grapefruit. Dissolve 115–200g/4–7oz/ generous ½–1 cup caster (superfine) sugar (the precise amount depends on the fruit's natural acidity) in 300ml/ ½ pint/1¼ cups boiling water, then mix it with the citrus juice and rind.

Top up to 1 litre/1¾ pints/ 4 cups with extra water or water and alcohol. Add enough alcohol to taste but don't be too generous or the granita will not freeze. Cool then chill.

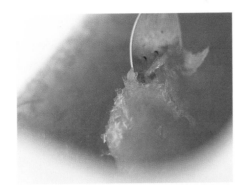

2 Pour the chilled mixture into a large plastic tub or similar freezerproof container. It should not be more than 2–2.5cm/¾–1in deep. Freeze in the coldest part of the freezer for 2 hours until it is mushy around the edges. Remove from the freezer and beat well with a fork to break up the ice crystals. Return to the freezer. Beat at 30 minute intervals for 2 hours until it has the texture of snow.

Not-fruit granitas

Coffee makes an excellent granita, and is easy to make. Pour hot, strong filtered coffee into a bowl or pan and stir in sugar to taste. For a ginger granita, infuse finely chopped fresh root ginger in boiling water, then sweeten it. Chocolate granita is made by mixing unsweetened cocoa powder to a smooth paste with a little boiling water and sweetening to taste, then gradually stirring in more boiling water. All these must be left to cool, then chilled in the refrigerator before being frozen.

Fruit-flavoured granita

To make a fruit-flavoured granita, purée berry fruits such as raspberries or strawberries, then sieve (strain) to remove the seeds. Alternatively, purée ripe peaches, then sieve to remove the skins. To make a melon granita, scoop the seeds out of orange- or green-fleshed melons, then purée the flesh. Peeled and seeded watermelon can be puréed in the same way, or the flesh can be puréed along with the seeds and then sieved afterwards.

ABOVE: *After puréeing fruits, always strain them to remove the skin and seeds.*

Serving and storing granitas
Coffee granita is classically served in a tumbler with whipped cream on top. Other types look pretty in tall glasses and decorated with fresh fruits, herb leaves and flowers. Because of its soft texture, a granita is best served as soon as it is made. Or try leaving it for a couple of hours in the freezer, beating once or twice more. If you must freeze one overnight, or longer, let it thaw slightly and beat really well with a fork before serving. The ice crystals will be smaller but the taste will be the same.

Dessert Sauces

From custard to fruit coulis, sauces add the finishing touch to your dessert. Some are very quick and easy, others take a little effort – but the results will be well worth it.

CLASSIC DESSERT SAUCES

These are the important recipes that should always be in any dessert-maker's repertoire.

Crème Anglaise

Here is the classic English custard – far superior to packet versions. It can be served hot or cold.

SERVES 4

1 vanilla pod (bean)
450ml/³⁄4 pint/1⁷⁄8 cups full cream (whole) milk
40g/1½ oz/3 tbsp caster (superfine) sugar
4 egg yolks

1 Split the vanilla pod with a sharp knife and place in a pan with the milk. Bring slowly to the boil.

2 Remove the pan from the heat, then cover and leave to infuse for 10 minutes before removing the pod.

3 Beat together the caster sugar and egg yolks until the mixture is thick, light and creamy.

4 Slowly pour the warm milk on to the egg mixture, stirring constantly until well mixed.

5 Transfer to the top of a double boiler or place the bowl over a pan of hot water. Stir constantly over a low heat for 10 minutes or until the mixture coats the back of the spoon. Remove from the heat immediately as curdling will occur if it is allowed to simmer.

6 Strain into a jug (pitcher) if serving hot or, if serving cold, strain into a bowl and cover the surface with baking parchment or clear film (plastic wrap).

Custard variation

Adding a little cornflour to the recipe will stabilize the egg and help to prevent curdling. This variation is simple to make.

SERVES 4–6

450ml/³⁄4 pint/scant 2 cups full cream (whole) milk
a few drops of vanilla extract
2 eggs plus 1 egg yolk
15–30ml/1–2 tbsp caster (superfine) sugar
15ml/1 tbsp cornflour (cornstarch)
30ml/2 tbsp water

1 Heat the milk with the vanilla extract and remove from the heat just as the milk comes to the boil.

2 Whisk the eggs and yolk in a bowl with the caster sugar until well combined but not frothy. In a separate bowl, blend the cornflour with the water and mix into the eggs. Whisk in a little of the hot milk, then mix in all the remaining milk.

3 Strain the egg and milk mixture back into the pan and heat gently, stirring frequently. Take care not to overheat the mixture or it will curdle.

4 Continue stirring until the custard thickens sufficiently to coat the back of a wooden spoon. Do not allow to boil or it will curdle. Serve immediately.

Sabayon

Serve this frothy sauce hot over steamed puddings or chill and serve cold with light dessert biscuits (cookies) or fruit. If serving hot, it must be served immediately as it will collapse if it is left to stand for any length of time.

SERVES 4–6

1 egg

2 egg yolks

75g/3oz/²/₃ cup caster (superfine) sugar

150ml/¹/₄ pint/²/₃ cups sweet white wine

finely grated rind and juice of 1 lemon

1 Whisk the egg, yolks and sugar until they are pale and thick.

2 Sit the bowl over a pan of hot (not boiling) water. Gradually add the wine and lemon juice, whisking vigorously.

3 Continue whisking until the mixture is thick enough to leave a trail when the whisk is lifted. Whisk in the lemon rind. If serving hot, serve immediately.

4 To serve cold, place over a bowl of iced water and whisk until chilled. Serve at once.

Brandy butter

This is traditionally served during the festive season in the UK with Christmas pudding and mince pies. It is, however, excellent served all year round: a good spoonful on a hot baked apple is delicious.

SERVES 6

100g/4oz/¹/₂ cup butter

100g/4oz/¹/₂ cup soft light brown sugar, icing (confectioners') or caster (superfine)

45ml/3 tbsp brandy

1 Cream the butter until very pale and soft. Beat in the sugar gradually until the mixture is smooth.

2 Add the brandy, a few drops at a time, beating constantly. Add enough for a good flavour but take care it does not curdle.

3 Pile the brandy butter into a small serving dish and allow to harden. Alternatively, spread on to foil and chill until firm, then cut the butter into shapes with small fancy cutters for serving.

Butterscotch Sauce

A deliciously sweet sauce that will be loved by adults and children alike! It is excellent served with pancakes or waffles, or can be used as a special topping to create a dessert out of simple vanilla ice cream.

SERVES 4–6

75g/3oz/6 tbsp butter
175g/6oz/3⁄4 cup soft dark brown sugar
175ml/6fl oz/3⁄4 cup evaporated milk
50g/2oz/1⁄2 cup hazelnuts

1 Melt the butter with the sugar in a heavy pan. Bring to the boil and boil, stirring, for 2 minutes. Cool for 5 minutes.

2 Heat the evaporated milk to just below boiling point, then gradually stir into the butter and sugar mixture. Cook over a low heat for 2 minutes, stirring frequently.

3 Spread the hazelnuts out on a baking sheet and toast them under a hot grill (broiler) until the skins become loose.

4 Put the nuts on to a clean dish towel and rub them briskly to remove the skins.

5 Chop the nuts roughly using a heavy knife and stir them into the sauce.

6 Serve hot, poured over scoops of vanilla ice cream and warm waffles or pancakes.

Orange Caramel Sauce

This sauce is excellent served over pancakes for a simple sweet dessert.

SERVES 4–6

25g/1oz/2 tbsp unsalted butter
50g/2oz/1⁄4 cup caster (superfine) sugar
juice of 2 oranges and 1⁄2 lemon

1 Melt the butter in a heavy pan. Stir in the caster sugar and cook until golden brown.

2 Add the orange and lemon juice and stir until the caramel has dissolved. Serve immediately.

Summer Berry Sauce

Another quick and tasty sauce to serve on pancakes or ice cream. Also great with fruity puddings. If serving for children, replace the liqueur with extra orange juice.

SERVES 4–6

25g/1oz/2 tbsp butter
50g/2oz/1⁄4 cup caster (superfine) sugar
juice of 2 oranges and grated rind of
**   1⁄2 orange**
350g/12oz/3 cups mixed summer berries
45ml/3 tbsp orange-flavoured liqueur

1 Melt the butter in a frying pan. Add the caster sugar and cook until golden in colour.

2 Add the orange juice and rind and cook until syrupy. Add the mixed summer berries and warm through.

3 Add the liqueur and set alight. Serve immediately.

Glossy Chocolate Sauce

Delicious poured over ice cream or on hot or cold desserts, this sauce also freezes well. Pour into a freezer-proof container, seal, and keep for up to three months. Thaw at room temperature before using.

SERVES 6

115g/4oz/½ cup caster (superfine) sugar
175g/6oz plain (semisweet) chocolate, broken into squares
30ml/2 tbsp unsalted butter
30ml/2 tbsp brandy or orange juice

1 Place the sugar and 60ml/4 tbsp of water in a pan and heat gently, stirring occasionally, until the sugar dissolves.

2 Stir in the chocolate, a few squares at a time, until melted, then add the butter in the same way. Do not allow the sauce to boil. Stir in the brandy or orange juice and serve warm.

Chocolate Fudge Sauce

This is a real treat if you're not counting calories. It is especially fabulous with scoops of good quality vanilla ice cream.

SERVES 6

150ml/¼ pint/⅔ cup double (heavy) cream
50g/2oz/4 tbsp butter
50g/2oz/¼ cup granulated (white) sugar
175g/6oz plain (semisweet) chocolate
30ml/2 tbsp brandy

1 Heat the double cream with the butter and sugar in the top of a double boiler or in a heatproof bowl set over a pan of hot (not boiling) water. Stir until smooth.

2 Break the plain chocolate into the cream mixture. Stir until it is melted and thoroughly combined.

3 Stir in the brandy a little at a time, then cool the sauce to room temperature before serving.

Chocolate Fudge Sauce variations
Try these variations on the classic sauce, which are great when used to match either a citrus- or coffee-based dessert respectively. Try serving poured over profiteroles for a truly indulgent dessert.

White Chocolate and Orange Sauce
• Replace the granulated (white) sugar with 40g/1½ oz/3 tbsp caster (superfine) sugar, the plain (semisweet) chocolate with white chocolate and the brandy with orange liqueur, and add the finely grated rind of 1 orange.
• Add the orange rind in step 1 with the cream, butter and sugar, and follow the recipe to the end using the substituted ingredients.

Coffee Chocolate Fudge Sauce
• Replace the granulated (white) sugar with soft light brown sugar and the brandy with coffee liqueur or dark rum, and add 15ml/1 tbsp coffee extract.
• Follow the recipe, using the substituted ingredients, and add the coffee extract at the end.

USING VANILLA PODS (BEANS)

Vanilla pods are often used in sweet dessert sauces – most commonly to flavour milk, cream or sugar before they are used to make the sauce – so it is worth knowing how to use them to their full potential.

Vanilla Infusions

1 To infuse vanilla flavour into milk or cream for a sauce, put the milk or cream in a pan, add the whole vanilla pod and heat gently over a low heat until the milk or cream is almost boiling.

2 At this point, remove the pan from the heat, cover and leave it to stand for 10 minutes.

3 Remove the vanilla pod. Rinse and dry the pod; it may be re-used several times so don't discard it.

4 To get maximum vanilla flavour into your sauce, use a sharp knife to slit the pod lengthways, then open it out.

5 Use the tip of the knife to scrape out the sticky black seeds inside. Add the seeds to the hot sauce.

Vanilla Sugar

Many dessert sauces benefit from the addition of vanilla-flavoured sugar. This is available commercially but it is easy to make your own.

1 To make vanilla sugar, simply bury a vanilla pod in a jar of white sugar. Cover tightly for a few weeks until the sugar takes on the vanilla flavour. Shake the jar occasionally.

SPEEDY SAUCES FOR TOPPING ICE CREAM

Store-cupboard (pantry) ingredients can be transformed into irresistible sauces to spoon on top of ice cream.

Marshmallow Melt

1 Melt 90g/3½oz marshmallows with 30ml/2 tbsp milk or cream in a pan. Add a little grated nutmeg and stir until smooth. Serve immediately.

Black Forest Sauce

1 Drain a can of black cherries, reserving the juice. Blend a little of the juice with a little arrowroot or cornflour (cornstarch).

2 Add the cornflour mixture to the rest of the juice in a pan. Heat, stirring, until boiling and slightly thickened, then add the cherries and a dash of Kirsch and heat through.

Raspberry Coulis

1 Purée some thawed frozen raspberries, with icing (confectioners') sugar to taste, then press through a sieve (strainer).

2 Blend a little cornflour (cornstarch) with some orange juice, and stir into the purée; cook for 2 minutes in a pan over a medium heat, stirring, until thick. Allow to cool.

Marmalade Whisky Sauce

1 Heat 60ml/4 tbsp chunky marmalade in a small pan with 30ml/2 tbsp whisky, until just melted.

2 Allow the sauce to bubble for a few seconds then spoon over ice cream and serve immediately.

PRESENTATION IDEAS

When you've made a delicious sauce for a special dessert, why not make more of it by using it for decoration on the plate, too? Individual slices of puddings, cakes or tarts, or baked fruit, look especially good served with sauce presented in this way. It will certainly provide a talking point for the dessert course of a dinner party, and it is surprisingly easy to create beautiful effects.

Marbling

Use this technique when you have two contrasting sauces of a similar thickness, such as a fruit purée with cream or thin fresh custard.

1 Spoon alternate spoonfuls of the two sauces on to a serving plate or shallow dish. Using a spoon, stir the sauces very lightly together, gently swirling them to create a pretty marbled effect.

Yin-Yang Sauces

This oriental pattern is ideal for two contrasting colours of purée or coulis, such as a raspberry and a mango fruit coulis. It is important to make sure that the flavours of the sauces complement one another.

1 Spoon a sauce on one side of a serving plate or shallow bowl. Add the second sauce to the other side.

2 Gently push the two sauces together with the spoon, swirling one around the other, to make a yin-yang shape.

Drizzling

1 Pour a smooth sauce or coulis into a container or tube with a fine pouring lip, or into a squeezy bottle with a small tip.

2 Drizzle the sauce in droplets or fine wavy lines on to the serving plate around the area where the dessert will sit to create an attractive pattern.

Feathering Hearts

1 Flood the serving plate with a thin layer of smooth dessert sauce, such as chocolate sauce or fruit purée.

2 Add small droplets of pouring (half-and-half) cream into it in a circular shape, spacing them at regular intervals.

3 Draw the tip of a small knife delicately and carefully through the droplets of cream, to drag each drop into a heart shape.

Piping Outlines

1 Spoon a small amount of fruit coulis or chocolate sauce into a piping (pastry) bag fitted with a plain writing nozzle.

2 Carefully pipe the outline of a simple shape, such as a circle or star, on to a serving plate.

3 Then, carefully use a teaspoon to spoon in more of the same sauce to fill all the space within the outline of the shape.

Index